WHAT PEOPLE ARE SAYIN

I first read Dr. King's "Letter from Birmingham Jail" as a freshman in high school. I have a vivid memory of being struck by his suggestion that perhaps the world is in "dire need of creative extremists" for love and the extension of justice, by those who would follow the biblical prophet Amos, Martin Luther, John Bunyan, Abraham Lincoln, and most importantly, the Lord Jesus Christ. The articulate vision and call to action contained in Dr. King's "Letter from Birmingham Jail" - for justice and love, for non-violent social activism, and for the involvement of all in seeing racial harmony and justice come in increasing measure in our world - remain a timely, challenging and important message for the 21st century. Many have read the letter. I earnestly pray this reprinting, along with helpful outline and index of significant quotations, will play a part to draw us again to the vision expressed by Dr. King, reflecting the vision of God himself for shalom in the world.

PROFESSOR MICHAEL B. KELLY
Assistant Professor of Old Testament
Westminster Theological Seminary

Americans have benefited from the faith and fortitude of Dr. Martin Luther King Jr., but often at a comfortable distance from the moral conscience and courage that were required to secure these benefits. From a dim and dusty jail cell, Dr. King challenged the leaders of the faith community as the custodians of Biblical Truth. His powerful thesis declared that when such leaders are void of the will to confront injustice with direct action, they have abandoned their Christian responsibility.

Dr. Peter Lillback, preeminent scholar, theologian, and historian, reminds us that Dr. King was not simply a great, gifted thinker. He was also an exceptional theologian and historian. *Annotations on a Letter That Changed the World From a Birmingham Jail* is an amazing exhibition of this fact.

REV. DR. HERBERT H. LUSK, II
Pastor, Greater Exodus Baptist Church, Philadelphia, PA
Founder and CEO, People For People, Inc.
Former Philadelphia Eagles Running Back

In making *Annotations on a Letter That Changed the World From a Birmingham Jail* available with his incisive editorial comments, Dr. Peter Lillback has rendered a great service to those around the world who seek reconciliation of people of all races. His intelligent approach provides added learning to issues of race long dividing humankind. This is a must read for Heads of State world wide, University and College leaders, State and Local governments, students and all those who have a yearning for peace and reconciliation.

We are indebted to Dr. Lillback for an unselfish act of service.

REV. DR. W. WILSON GOODE, SR.
Mayor of Philadelphia, 1984-1992

"Letter from a Birmingham Jail" is inspiring and one of a kind. There is little doubt that Martin Luther King Jr. was a spiritual giant. His Letter not only deals with theology, it encompasses ethics, law, history, society, and literary artistry. It is always a part of my philosophy of religion classes.

Its many well-chosen phrases echo in the mind: "freedom is never voluntarily given," "the cup of endurance runs over," "flowing with floods of blood," his metaphorical comparison of the church as either a thermometer or thermostat, and sister Pollard's memorably incorrect grammar, "My feets is tired, but my soul is rested." He was both an eyewitness and one who suffered the demeaning cruelty delivered to the Blacks. To the moderate white church his message was "wake-up." His Letter is Christianity in action.

Dr. Lillback's insightful citations and annotations add significance to the origin and meaning of the Letter. It is of value to see the slight changes made between the original and "polished" versions. Who would guess that this profound writing began on the margins of a newspaper? In the twenty-first century, who would know that Birmingham, aka "Bombingham," was the most segregated city in America, or that there were 48 unsolved bombings between 1948 and 1957? Who would know that "Bull" Connors had perpetuated segregation for twenty-two years as the sheriff?

This document should be read and reread by every pastor and Christian without exception, especially those who say that social and political issues are not their talking points.

BRUCE WEBER, STD, PHD
Adjunct Instructor
Brandman/Chapman University

ANNOTATIONS ON A LETTER THAT CHANGED THE WORLD FROM A BIRMINGHAM JAIL

ANNOTATIONS ON A LETTER THAT CHANGED THE WORLD FROM A BIRMINGHAM JAIL

"INJUSTICE ANYWHERE IS A
THREAT TO JUSTICE EVERYWHERE."

By
Peter A. Lillback
President, The Providence Forum
President, Westminster Theological Seminary

THE PROVIDENCE FORUM PRESS
2013

Reprinted by arrangement with The Heirs to the Estate of Martin Luther King Jr., c/o
Writers House as agent for the proprietor New York, NY.
*Copyright 1963 Dr. Martin Luther King Jr; copyright renewed
1991 Coretta Scott King.*

Annotations by Peter A. Lillback
Copyright Peter A. Lillback 2013

 PROVIDENCE FORUM PRESS

Annotations on a Letter That Changed the World From a Birmingham Jail

Copyright ©2013 Peter Lillback. All rights reserved.

ISBN: 9780984765416

Cover and Interior Design:
Roark Creative, www.roarkcreative.com

Printed in the United States of America.

Providence Forum Press
The Providence Forum
2002 Renaissance Blvd., Suite 230
King of Prussia, PA 19406
www.providenceforum.org

Annotations on a Letter That Changed the World From a Birmingham Jail
is dedicated to all those who
long to see the reconciliation of people of all races in
the spirit of Jesus' Golden Rule:

"Do unto others as you would have them do unto you."
Matthew 7:12

TABLE OF CONTENTS

ANNOTATIONS ON A LETTER THAT CHANGED THE WORLD FROM A BIRMINGHAM JAIL

BY DR. PETER A. LILLBACK

Martin Luther King, Jr. died on April 4, 1968 as a martyr for the civil rights cause to which he had pledged his life. As an ordained African-American Baptist Pastor, a trained theologian, a student of social forces and movements, he was well prepared to write a manifesto for the civil rights movement. His arrest in Birmingham Alabama in April 1963 gave him the opportunity to produce this brilliantly persuasive and spiritually moving epistle. Dr. King received The Nobel Peace Prize the following year in 1964 for his leadership of the civil rights cause in America.

Although this text was produced as a letter intended for reading, the reader would benefit, along with others, to hear it read aloud. For Martin Luther King's *Letter from Birmingham Jail*, displays the power and rhetoric of a reformer's sermon. Dr. King not only here reflects the power and conviction that characterized his great Protestant namesake, but like the Apostle Paul, Dr. King discovers that there is a special persuasiveness and emotional power in a prison epistle reverberating in the context of an unjust arrest for a just cause.

The form of the message is both an apology in the classic sense of a defense of the propriety of one's criticized or wrongly judged actions, and a jeremiad, or a bitter complaint against conduct that is unworthy of a group of people with whom one is associated.

The general themes Dr. King develops include:

- The defense of his direct action strategy.
- The method of determining whether a law is just.
- Disappointment with white moderates and the white church communities.
- A discussion of extremism in the struggle for racial justice.

- The blessings of the American heritage of liberty in terms of the black American.
- True heroism in the face of the police efforts for order and the demonstrators' efforts for justice.
- Hopes for brotherhood as a result of the establishment of civil rights.

Following this introduction, I have incorporated an outline of the text into the text itself. These headings will assist the reader in understanding, and will also aid in quickly finding key ideas of Dr. King's argument. They should not be read if the text is read aloud. Nor should they be considered part of the original text. Similarly, the endnotes are added for clarity and to identify the sources on the concepts which Dr. King used and to which he alluded. They too are not part of his *Letter*. I have also compiled two indices of Dr. King's *Letter*. The first is an Index of Significant Quotations. The second is a Topical Index of Biblical, Theological, Philosophical and Historical References that flow from my analysis of his work.

Dr. King described the historical context and circumstances of his *Letter* with a brief prefatory note that is given below.

> AUTHOR'S NOTE: This response to a published statement by eight fellow clergymen from Alabama[1] (Bishop C. C. J. Carpenter[2], Bishop Joseph A. Durick[3], Rabbi Hilton L. Grafman[4], Bishop Paul Hardin[5], Bishop Holan B. Harmon[6], the Reverend George M. Murray[7], the Reverend Edward V. Ramage[8] and the Reverend Earl Stallings[9]) was composed under somewhat constricting circumstance. Begun on the margins of the newspaper in which the statement appeared while I was in jail, the letter was continued on scraps of writing paper supplied by a friendly Negro trusty, and concluded on a pad my attorneys were eventually permitted to leave me. Although the text remains in substance unaltered, I have indulged in the author's prerogative of polishing it for publication.

Thus Dr. King's *Letter* directly answers the clergymen's statement and he directly and indirectly refers to them in the *Letter*.[10] The historical contexts of the clergymen's letter and Dr. King's response have been well summarized by news reports.[11]

Finally, Dr. King states that he subsequently "polished" the work for publication. The text used here is his first unedited version of the *Letter*. His final and minimal edits to improve his work can be found in the last section of this book that presents Dr. King's *Letter* without the outline and annotations. There his final edits are identified by endnotes. Regardless of the version read, the breadth of knowledge, the penetrating insight, the grasp of historical thinkers and their specific words revealed in his letter, mostly written in the barren surroundings of a jail cell, are nothing less than a testimony to genius.

We will all be wiser and better if we take the time to learn from this remarkable scholar, passionate preacher, social change agent and embodiment of his people. Dr. King's legacy should be celebrated by all Americans regardless of color, class or creed!

Dr. Peter Lillback
President
The Providence Forum

INTRODUCTION NOTES

[1] The following statement has sometimes been called "A Call for Unity" and the signatories referred to themselves as "The Committee of Reconciliation".

PUBLIC STATEMENT BY EIGHT ALABAMA CLERGYMEN, April 12, 1963

We the undersigned clergymen are among those who, in January, issued "An Appeal for Law and Order and Common Sense," in dealing with racial problems in Alabama. We expressed understanding that honest convictions in racial matters could properly be pursued in the courts, but urged that decisions of those courts should in the meantime be peacefully obeyed. Since that time there had been some evidence of increased forbearance and a willingness to face facts. Responsible citizens have undertaken to work on various problems which cause racial friction and unrest. In Birmingham, recent public events have given indication that we all have opportunity for a new constructive and realistic approach to racial problems. However, we are now confronted by a series of demonstrations by some of our Negro citizens, directed and led in part by outsiders. We recognize the natural impatience of people who feel that their hopes are slow in being realized. But we are convinced that these demonstrations are unwise and untimely.

We agree rather with certain local Negro leadership which has called for honest and open negotiation of racial issues in our area. And we believe this kind of facing of issues can best be accomplished by citizens of our own metropolitan area, white and Negro, meeting with their knowledge and experience of the local situation. All of us need to face that responsibility and find proper channels for its accomplishment.

Just as we formerly pointed out that "hatred and violence have no sanction in our religious and political traditions," we also point out that such actions as incite to hatred and violence, however technically peaceful those actions may be, have not contributed to the resolution of our local problems. We do not believe that these days of new hope are days when extreme measures are justified in Birmingham.

We commend the community as a whole, and the local news media and law enforcement in particular, on the calm manner in which these demonstrations have been handled. We urge the public to continue to show restraint should the demonstrations continue, and the law enforcement officials to remain calm and continue to protect our city from violence.

We further strongly urge our own Negro community to withdraw support from these demonstrations, and to unite locally in working peacefully for a better Birmingham. When rights are consistently denied, a cause should be pressed in the courts and in negotiations among local leaders, and not in the streets. We appeal to both our white and Negro citizenry to observe the principles of law and order and common sense. (available on www.Stanford.edu)

C. C. J. Carpenter, D.D., LL.D., *Bishop of Alabama*
Joseph A. Durick, D.D., *Auxiliary Bishop, Diocese of Mobile, Birmingham*
Rabbi Hilton L. Grafman, *Temple Emanu-El, Birmingham, Alabama*
Bishop Paul Hardin, *Bishop of the Alabama-West Florida Conference*
Bishop Nolan B. Harmon, *Bishop of the North Alabama Conference of the Methodist Church*
George M. Murray, D.D., LL.D., *Bishop Coadjutor, Episcopal Diocese of Alabama*
Edward V. Ramage, *Moderator, Synod of the Alabama Presbyterian Church in the United States*

Earl Stallings, *Pastor, First Baptist Church, Birmingham, Alabama*

[2] C. C. J. Carpenter, D.D., LL.D. was the Episcopal Bishop of Alabama. We gain insights into Bishop Carpenter from an essay by the Rev. Douglas Carpenter (retired, rector of St. Stephen's Episcopal Church, Birmingham, Ala.) about his father, Bishop C.C.J. Carpenter (The Episcopal Church Web site, July 13, 2007):

> I grew up in Birmingham in the '30s and '40s. It was not peaceful. It was a very tough steel-producing city, covered with smoke and soot. There were frequent murders.
>
> My father, C. C. J. Carpenter, was the bishop of the Alabama Diocese from 1938, when I had just turned 5, until 1968. In 1951, a parish in Mobile wanted to start a parochial school. He gave his approval only when they agreed it could be integrated. Actions such as this put him on the hit list of the White Citizens Council and the Ku Klux Klan. He got frequent hate threats by phone.
>
> After the Brown vs. Board of Education decision in 1954, racial events began to heat up in Birmingham, and he was quite aware of white people in Birmingham and other parts of the state who were capable of murder.
>
> I remember how happy he was when a local law was passed forbidding people to wear masks in public. He thought this would really set the Klan back. He thought of them as cowards who were afraid to show their faces. Another local law was passed forbidding public marches without a permit. This was to stop the Klan and the White Citizens Council. This was long before the civil rights marches....

Bishop Carpenter and the other pastors Dr. King identified in the *Letter* were by and large racial progressives who were attempting to keep their congregations united. They are the focus of a book by S. Jonathan Bass, *Blessed Are the Peacemakers: Martin Luther King, Jr., Eight White Religious Leaders, and the "Letter from Birmingham Jail,"* Baton Rouge, Louisiana State University Press, 2001.

[3] On June 28, 1994, Wolfgang Saxon of the New York Times reported on the death of Bishop Durick: "Bishop Joseph Durick, 79, Civil Rights Advocate":

Bishop Joseph Aloysius Durick, who emerged as a strong voice for civil rights in the segregated South despite opposition from his tradition-bound congregation and other members of the clergy, died on Sunday at his home in Bessemer, Alabama according to the Roman Catholic Diocese of Nashville, which he served as Bishop from 1969 to 1975. He was 79. ... prodded by the Second Vatican Council and the moral suasion of the Rev. Dr. Martin Luther King Jr., he came to have a troubled conscience on civil rights, even though his views were shared at first by few of his white peers.

In Tennessee, Bishop Durick put in place decrees of Vatican II that were intended to eliminate social inequities. He drew national notice with his stand for an end to racial divisions and for compassion for the poor and others left out of the mainstream, a position that drew protests in his diocese.

[4] Rabbi Milton Louis Grafman (1907 - 1995) led Temple Emanu-El in Birmingham from 1941 to 1975. He joined the clergymen that sought to defuse racial tensions during the lead-up of Dr. King's non-violent protests. He and the clergy criticized the city's segregation policies as well as Governor George Wallace's 1963 inaugural speech that called for "segregation now, segregation forever." Nevertheless, the clergymen troubled Dr. King by their call to delay demonstrations and to wait for the courts to act against racial discrimination. The Rev. Douglas Carpenter, retired, was rector of St. Stephen's Episcopal Church, Birmingham, Ala. Writing about his father, Bishop C.C.J. Carpenter, Rev. Carpenter says of Rabbi Grafman, "At my first Diocesan Convention in Alabama after ordination, 1961, I was amazed at the anger of some of the white delegates. At times it looked as though they wanted to physically abuse my "liberal" father....At that time [1974], Rabbi Milton Grafman was the only one addressed in the *Letter from Birmingham Jail* who was still active in Birmingham. I went to talk with him about the '60s. His first comment was, "I truly think Birmingham might have been burned to the ground if it hadn't been for your father." (July 13, 2007, The Episcopal Church Web site.)

[5] Paul Hardin, Jr. (1903-1996) was elected in 1960 as Bishop of the Alabama-West Florida Annual Conference of the Methodist Church. Bishop Hardin was installed as president of the United Methodist Church's Council of Bishops on April 15, 1971 in San Antonio, Texas. Garrow writes in his review of Bass, "While Bass...wrongly seeks to dismiss the transformative impact of

Martin Luther King's involvement in Birmingham, the best sections of *Blessed Are the Peacemakers* are those that describe how being among the recipients of King's famous 'Letter' did have a reformative if not transformative effect upon some of the more moderate of the eight clergymen. When Bass asked Methodist Bishop Paul Hardin, Jr., about King's Letter in 1992, Hardin replied that 'I think most of his arguments were right. White ministers should have taken a more active role.'" (p. 30.)

[6] Nolan Bailey Harmon was born in 1892 in Mississippi and died in 1993, living to be over 100 years old. He was the son, grandson and great-grandson of Methodist Preachers. He was elected in 1956 to be the Bishop of The United Methodist Church. Bishop Harmon, the oldest out of the eight white clergymen, along with fellow-Methodist Bishop Paul Hardin Jr., released a statement calling on African-Americans to stop taking part in demonstrations initiated by the Rev. Dr. Martin Luther King Jr., calling King's actions *"unwise and untimely."* It was this statement that provoked Dr. King, causing him to write his *Letter from Birmingham Jail.* In his 1983 autobiography, Bishop Harmon referred to the letter as a *"propaganda move."* David Garrow, p. 30, writes, "Bass also acknowledges that Methodist Bishop Nolan B. Harmon's 'position on segregation never evolved,' but Bass is more outspoken in recognizing what he terms Harmon's 'outstanding contribution to Methodism' and in repeatedly decrying the 'crusading mentality and sense of moral superiority of many white northerners.'"

[7] George Mosley Murray (1919-2006) was an Episcopalian Bishop and the youngest of the eight Alabama clergymen who wrote "A Call For Unity". During the Civil Rights Movement Murray and his wife, Elizabeth Malcolm Murray, were active in the civil rights efforts, for which they were criticized for being too involved or not involved enough.

[8] Edward V. Ramage was the Moderator of the Synod of the Alabama Presbyterian Church in the United States. He was also pastor of the First Presbyterian Church of Birmingham.

[9] Rev. Earl Stallings (1916-2006) was praised by the Reverend Martin Luther King Jr. in his *Letter from Birmingham Jail.* Stallings angered members of his white congregation by opening his doors to black worshipers. One of the blacks allowed in was the civil rights leader Andrew Young.

On March 7, 2006, the *New York Times News Service* reported "Pastor praised by jailed King: White Baptist minister integrated a service at his Birmingham, Ala., church during the civil rights era":

> Rev. Earl Stallings, a prominent Baptist pastor in Birmingham, Ala., who in 1963 risked the rejection of his own white congregation, and worse, by seating African-American worshipers among them

at his Easter service amid the city's erupting racial antagonisms, has died in Lakeland, Fla. He was 89.

Rev. Stallings was pastor of the First Baptist Church when the Rev. Martin Luther King Jr. wrote his impassioned "Letter From Birmingham Jail," in which he presented his view on civil disobedience to unjust laws. King also appealed to white members of the clergy to support the civil rights movement and chastised some white moderates as being "more devoted to `order' than to justice." He mentioned Rev. Stallings by name as one of the few who took the side of justice.

Garrow writes in his review of Bass, "And far and away the most powerful and moving section of Bass's book is his treatment of Baptist Reverend Earl Stallings, who welcomed Black worshippers into his First Baptist Church at the height of the 1963 protest and who 'publicly blamed Birmingham's white churches for much of the climate of unrest in the city.'"(p. 30.)

[10] Please refer to the Outline of the *Letter* to see references by Dr. King to the clergymen and their statement:

[11] Cary McMullen reported in *The Ledger*, March 19, 2006, "The Cost of Courage: Pastor Suffered for Attempts to Make Peace Between Two Historic Forces":

> ..."If we can crack Birmingham," the Rev. Martin Luther King Jr. reportedly said, "I'm convinced we can crack the South." Caught in the middle was a large body of white moderates who knew change was inevitable but hoped it could be accomplished gradually and peacefully. They included many clergymen, and eight in particular would serve as representatives of them all. The Committee of Reconciliation, they sometimes called themselves.

The eight would be addressed in one of the most important documents in American history, and one of them would be singled out by name. He's there, in one sentence: "I commend you, Rev. Stallings, for your Christian stand on this past Sunday, in welcoming Negroes to your service on a non-segregated basis."

The document was King's *Letter from Birmingham Jail*. The man he commended was the Rev. Earl Stallings, pastor of First Baptist Church. The Sunday was Easter Day, April 14, 1963.

DR. MARTIN LUTHER KING JR.'S ORIGINAL UNEDITED LETTER FROM BIRMINGHAM JAIL

I. Introduction: An Answer to an Open Letter Calling Dr. King's Work "Unwise and Untimely."

My dear Fellow Clergymen,[12]

While confined here in the Birmingham City Jail, I came across your recent statement calling our present activities "unwise and untimely."[13] Seldom, if ever, do I pause to answer criticism of my work and ideas. If I sought to answer all the criticisms that cross my desk, my secretaries would be engaged in little else in the course of the day and I would have no time for constructive work. But since I feel that you are men of genuine goodwill and your criticisms are sincerely set forth, I would like to answer your statement in what I hope will be patient and reasonable terms.

[12] See notes 1-11 in Introduction.
[13] See note 1 in Introduction.

II. A Defense of Direct Action.
A. Why Dr. King is in Birmingham Since He Is from Atlanta.
1. The Southern Christian Leadership Conference Was Asked to Help Address Injustice in Alabama, and Has Responded, Bringing Dr. King to Birmingham.

I think I should give the reason for my being in Birmingham[14], since you have been influenced by the argument of "outsiders coming in."[15] I have the honor of serving as president of the Southern Christian Leadership Conference,[16] an organization operating in every Southern state with headquarters in Atlanta, Georgia. We have some eighty-five affiliate organizations all across the South -- one being the Alabama Christian Movement for Human Rights.[17]

Whenever necessary and possible we share staff, educational, and financial resources with our affiliates. Several months ago our local affiliate here in Birmingham invited us to be on call to engage in a nonviolent direct action program if such were deemed necessary. We readily consented and when the hour came we lived up to our promises. So I am here, along with several members of my staff, because we were invited here.

[14] Birmingham, a highly segregated city of about a quarter of a million inhabitants in the 1960's, prohibited the mixing of races in most community contexts. David J. Garrow elucidates the painful realities of the racial struggles there in "Many Birminghams: Taking Segregationists Seriously", pp. 26-32:

> Birmingham, Alabama, has symbolized the violent intensity of southern white segregationist opposition to the Black freedom struggle ever since city Public Safety Director Eugene "Bull" Connor used snarling police dogs and high-pressure fire hoses against Black demonstrators in April and May, 1963. When four young girls were killed in a Ku Klux Klan terror bombing of Birmingham's Sixteenth Street Baptist Church just four months later, the city's reputation was sealed for decades to come. But Birmingham in the 1960s was far less unique than many people nowadays imagine, and a quartet of new books reveals that Birmingham was far more representative of the white South than most people would care to remember.
>
> Southern recalcitrance at desegregating bus seats, lunch counters, and public facilities ranging from restrooms to golf courses was virtually region-wide until congressional passage of the public accommodations provisions in the Civil Rights Act of 1964 finally resolved such issues once and for all. But even in the midst of a region-wide revolt against Black activism and federal authority, contemporary news coverage presented Birmingham as the southern archetype for both barbarous law enforcement and unrestrained Klansmen.

[15] The Southern Christian Leadership Conference conducted nationwide efforts to support civil rights with which Dr. King cooperated. Their cooperation with the civil rights activities in Birmingham were viewed by many as disrupters of the city's peace and destabilizing agitators from outside the community.

[16] From 1957, the Southern Christian Leadership Conference (SCLC) sought to organize the civil rights efforts in the segregated southern states. Dr. King coordinated the African-American churches to maximize the impact of non-violent protests against racial injustices.

[17] The Alabama Christian Movement for Human Rights, (ACMHR) was organized under the leadership of the Rev. Fred Shuttlesworth in Birmingham, Alabama, on June 5, 1956, after the National Association for the Advancement of Colored People (NAACP) was outlawed in Alabama.

2. I Am in Birmingham Because Injustice Is Here. I Must Respond to the Macedonian Call for Aid As the Apostle Paul Did by Carrying Forth the Gospel of Freedom.

I am here because I have basic organizational ties here. Beyond this, I am in Birmingham because injustice is here. Just as the eighth century prophets left their little villages and carried their "thus saith the Lord" far beyond the boundaries of their home town, [18] and just as the Apostle Paul left his little village of Tarsus and carried the gospel of Jesus Christ to practically every hamlet and city of the Graeco-Roman world, [19] I too am compelled to carry the gospel of freedom[20] beyond my particular home town. Like Paul, I must constantly respond to the Macedonian call for aid. [21]

[18] This would likely include the Old Testament prophets Obadiah (855-840?BC), Jonah (785-775 BC), Amos (760-750 BC), Hosea (760-750 BC), Isaiah (740-681 BC). The prophet Amos, for example, was from Tekoa a small town in the southern kingdom of Judah near Bethlehem and about eleven miles from Jerusalem. He was sent as Dr. King says, "beyond the boundaries of [his] hometown" to carry the "'thus saith the Lord'" of the coming judgment of God upon the northern kingdom of Israel. This can be seen in Amos chapters 2 through 7. Amos 3:1-2 says, "Hear this word the Lord has spoken against you, O people of Israel—against the whole family I brought up out of Egypt: 'You only have I chosen of all the families of the

earth; therefore I will punish you for all your sins.'" (All biblical citations are from the NIV unless otherwise noted).

[19] The story of the apostle Paul is found in Acts chapters 8-28 as well as in his New Testament epistles. Acts 9:11 states that Paul was from Tarsus. Paul's commission to go to the "far corners of the Greco-Roman world" is expressed in Acts 26:15-18, "Then I asked, 'Who are you, Lord?' "'I am Jesus, whom you are persecuting,' the Lord replied. Now get up and stand on your feet. I have appeared to you to appoint you as a servant and as a witness of what you have seen of me and what I will show you. I will rescue you from your own people and from the Gentiles. I am sending you to them to open their eyes and turn them from darkness to light, and from the power of Satan to God, so that they may receive forgiveness of sins and a place among those who are sanctified by faith in me." In fulfillment of this calling, he conducted missionary journeys that are reported in the book of Acts.

[20] This is an allusion to Jesus' and Paul's teaching. Jesus said in John 8:31-32, "If you hold to my teaching you are really my disciples. Then you will know the truth, and the truth will set you free." Paul said in Galatians 5:1, "It is for freedom that Christ has set us free. Stand firm, then, and do not let yourselves be burdened again by a yoke of slavery." 2 Corinthians 3:17 teaches, "Now the Lord is the Spirit, and where the Spirit of the Lord is, there is freedom." Paul recognizes that this spiritual freedom also implies the value of civil freedom in 1 Corinthians 7:20-23, "Each one should remain in the situation which he was in when God called him. Were you a slave when you were called? Don't let it trouble you—although if you can gain your freedom, do so. For he who was a slave when he was called by the Lord is the Lord's freedman; similarly, he who was a free man when he was called is Christ's slave. You were bought at a price; do not become slaves of men." This "gospel of freedom" asserted by Dr. King is based on the Old Testament messianic prophecy of Isaiah 61:1-2, "The Spirit of the Sovereign Lord is on me, because the Lord has anointed me to preach good news to the poor. He has sent me to bind up the brokenhearted, to proclaim freedom for the captives and release from darkness for the prisoners, to proclaim the year of the Lord's favor and the day of vengeance of our God, to comfort all who mourn."

[21] The figure of speech, the "Macedonian call for aid", used by Dr. King is based on Paul's calling by the Holy Spirit to bring the gospel to Macedonia and so help the European gentiles to know the good news as seen in Acts 16:10. It is an especially apt metaphor since

it presents a biblical antidote to the charge of being an outside agitator, or as Dr. King says, "outsiders coming in". Just as Paul was called to enter Macedonia to bring help to the needy, so Dr. King was called to come to Birmingham to bring good news to the poor and downtrodden there.

3. Injustice Anywhere Is a Threat to Justice Everywhere. The Interrelatedness of All of American Life.

Moreover, I am cognizant of the interrelatedness of all communities and states. I cannot sit idly by in Atlanta and not be concerned about what happens in Birmingham. Injustice anywhere is a threat to justice everywhere. We are caught in an inescapable network of mutuality tied in a single garment of destiny. Whatever affects one directly affects all indirectly. Never again can we afford to live with the narrow, provincial "outside agitator" idea. Anyone who lives inside the United States can never be considered an outsider anywhere in this country.[22]

[22] Dr. King's piercing rhetoric not only reflects the lofty ideal of the first name of our country, "United" States, but it also reflects the Constitutional ideal (Article IV, Section 1.) of each state honoring the "full faith and credit" of the other states. This idealism continues to inspire many as the world becomes more and more a global village due to the power of technology, instant communication and rapid transportation. But it also reflects the spiritual ideal of the church as the Body of Christ as taught by Paul in 1 Corinthians 12. 1 Corinthians 12:25-26 states, "so that there should be no division in the body, but that its parts should have equal concern for each other. If one part suffers, every part suffers with it; if one part is honored, every part rejoices with it."

4. Criticism of the Demonstrations Should Not Be Guilty of a Superficial Social Analysis That Deals Merely with Effects and Does Not Grapple with the Underlying Causes. They Are Unfortunate, But Necessary.

You deplore the demonstrations that are presently taking place in Birmingham. But I am sorry that your statement did not express a similar concern for the conditions that brought the demonstrations into being. I am sure that each of you would want to go beyond the superficial social analyst who looks merely at effects, and does not grapple with underlying causes. I would not hesitate to say that it is unfortunate that so-called demonstrations are taking place in Birmingham at this time, but I would say in more emphatic terms that it is even more unfortunate that the white power structure of this city left the Negro community with no other alternative.

II.

B. The Birmingham Campaign Has Followed the Four Steps of a Nonviolent Campaign.

In any nonviolent campaign[23] there are four basic steps: [24]

(1) Collection of the facts to determine whether injustices are alive;

(2) Negotiation;

(3) Self-purification; [25]

and (4) Direct action. [26]

We have gone through all of these steps in Birmingham.

---

[23] On September 1, 1958, Dr. King published an article entitled, "My Pilgrimage to Nonviolence" in *Fellowship*. It was an abridged version of the sixth chapter of his book, *Stride Toward Freedom* (New York: Harper and Brothers, 1958). In presenting the influences on his thought as he developed his conception of nonviolent activism he especially underscores the impact of Mahatma Gandhi's writings:

> Dr. Johnson had just returned from a trip to India, and, to my great interest, he spoke of the life and teachings of Mahatma Gandhi. His message was so profound and electrifying that I left the meeting and bought a half-dozen books on Gandhi's life and works.
>
> Like most people, I had heard of Gandhi, but I had never studied him seriously. As I read I became deeply fascinated by his campaigns of nonviolent resistance. I was particularly moved by the Salt March to the Sea and his numerous fasts. The whole concept of "Satyagraha" (*Satya* is truth which equals love and *agraha* is force: "Satyagraha," therefore, means truth-force or love force) was profoundly significant to me. As I delved deeper into the philosophy of Gandhi my skepticism concerning the power of love gradually diminished, and I came to see for the first time its potency in the area of social reform....The intellectual and moral satisfaction

that I failed to gain from the utilitarianism of Bentham and Mill, the revolutionary methods of Marx and Lenin, the social-contracts theory of Hobbes, the "back to nature" optimism of Rousseau, the superman philosophy of Nietzsche, I found in the nonviolent resistance philosophy of Gandhi. I came to feel that this was the only morally and practically sound method open to oppressed people in their struggle for freedom. (*The Papers of Martin Luther King*, Vol. IV, p. 478.)

[24] In *Stride Toward Freedom*, Dr. King outlines six principles of nonviolent confrontation: (1.) Nonviolence is not passive, but requires courage; (2.) Nonviolence seeks reconciliation, not defeat of an adversary; (3.) Nonviolent action is directed at eliminating evil, not destroying an evil-doer; (4.) A willingness to accept suffering for the cause, if necessary, but never to inflict it; (5.) A rejection of hatred, animosity or violence of the spirit, as well as refusal to commit physical violence; and (6.) Faith that justice will prevail.

[25] A foundational premise of Dr. King's understanding of active resistance and civil disobedience is Self-purification, which is an inner spiritual cleansing of the heart from selfishness, anger, and motivations toward violence. By such self-purification one becomes ready for nonviolent confrontation.

[26] See note 24. Direct action is a type of civil rights protest which was developed by Dr. King with the goal to end the racial injustices that were rampant in legalized segregation. It is a form of political protest that is confrontational in nature with activities that can theoretically range from the non-violent variety practiced by Dr. King to the overt violence perpetrated by guerrilla warfare. Dr. King's non-violent direct action employed marches, strikes, sit-ins, demonstrations, and various forms of peaceful civil disobedience against what were believed to be unjust laws.

Step 1. Racial Injustices Exist in Birmingham.

There can be no gainsaying of the fact that racial injustice engulfs this community. Birmingham is probably the most thoroughly segregated city in the United States. Its ugly record of police brutality is known in every section of this country. Its unjust treatment of Negroes in the courts is a notorious reality. There have been more unsolved bombings of Negro homes and churches in Birmingham than any city in this nation. [27] These are the hard, brutal, and unbelievable facts. On the basis of these conditions Negro leaders sought to negotiate with the city fathers. But the political leaders consistently refused to engage in good faith negotiation.

[27] Tragically, Birmingham was often referred to as "Bombingham" since there were 48 unsolved racial bombings in the city between 1948 and 1957. There were more than 40 unsolved bombings during the 1960s. David J. Garrow's review, "Many Birminghams: Taking Segregationists Seriously", pp. 26-32 considers, Diane McWhorter's *Carry Me Home, Birmingham, Alabama: The Climactic Battle of the Civil Rights Revolution*, (New York, Simon & Schuster, 2001). He writes,

> Diane McWhorter's *Carry Me Home* brings an intensely personal perspective to Birmingham's year of infamy. As a ten-year-old white girl who had been born into one of the city's most privileged families, "I knew nothing of what was happening downtown." Even five years later, despite the fact that her ne'er-do-well father presented himself to his family as an active Klan sympathizer, "I was more worried that he was going to bring social shame on the family than I was worried about the morality of what he was doing."
>
> Only in her late twenties did McWhorter develop an active interest in what had transpired in her hometown two decades earlier, and in part her interest grew out of her fear that her father's professed friendship with Birmingham's most notorious Klansman, Robert E. "Dynamite Bob" Chambliss, might mean that her father had been personally involved in the city's most heinous crime. "I know Chambliss didn't bomb the church because I was with him that day" in September 1963, Martin McWhorter told his daughter in 1982.

Step 2. Failed Negotiations: We Were the Victims of a Broken Promise.

Then came the opportunity last September to talk with some of the leaders of the economic community. In these negotiating sessions certain promises were made by the merchants -- such as the promise to remove the humiliating racial signs from the stores. On the basis of these promises Rev. Shuttlesworth[28] and the leaders of the Alabama Christian Movement for Human Rights[29] agreed to call a moratorium on any type of demonstrations. As the weeks and months unfolded we realized that we were the victims of a broken promise. The signs remained.

[28] A leader in the ACMHR and the SCLC, Fred Shuttlesworth, pastor of Bethel Baptist Church, guided the efforts in Birmingham for racial equality. He brought Dr. King to Birmingham in 1963 for the epic civil rights battle. A bomb was detonated under Shuttlesworth's house but he emerged unharmed. In 1963, he developed the strategy for the Birmingham Campaign. He issued the "Birmingham Manifesto" that declared, "We act today in full concert with our Hebraic-Christian tradition, the laws of morality and the Constitution of our nation … We appeal to the citizenry of Birmingham, Negro and white, to join us in this witness for decency, morality, self-respect and human dignity." Bishop C.C.J. Carpenter (The Episcopal Church Web site, July 13, 2007) notes:

> Black and white leaders often met in my father's office in the early '60s. At one meeting, my father said to the Rev. Fred Shuttlesworth, clearly the most effective leader among the black community, "Fred, what you want to accomplish could take 50 years." I still think it was an inappropriate statement at the time, but unfortunately it was true.
>
> I saw Dr. Shuttlesworth at a political gathering in Birmingham a few years ago. He said to me, "Oh, yes, I knew your father well. We disagreed on a few things." Then, in a very moving way, he said, "But we loved each other."

[29] See note 17 above.

Step 3. Preparing for Direct Action by Self-Purification: "Able to Accept blows without retaliating?" "Able to endure the ordeal of jail?"

As in so many experiences of the past we were confronted with blasted hopes, and the dark shadow of a deep disappointment settled upon us. So we had no alternative except that of preparing for direct action, whereby we would present our very bodies as a means of laying our case before the conscience of the local and national community. We were not unmindful of the difficulties involved. So we decided to go through a process of self-purification. We started having workshops on nonviolence and repeatedly asked ourselves the questions, "Are you able to accept blows without retaliating?" "Are you able to endure the ordeals of jail?"

We decided to set our direct-action program around the Easter season, realizing that with the exception of Christmas, this was the largest shopping period of the year. Knowing that a strong economic withdrawal program would be the by-product of direct action, we felt that this was the best time to bring pressure on the merchants for the needed changes.

Step 4. Several Postponements Were Endured and Direct-action Could No Longer Be Delayed.

Then it occurred to us that the March election[30] was ahead, and so we speedily decided to postpone action until after election day. When we discovered that Mr. Connor [31] was in the run-off, we decided again to postpone action so that the demonstrations could not be used to cloud the issues. At this time we agreed to begin our nonviolent witness the day after the run-off.

This reveals that we did not move irresponsibly into direct action. We too wanted to see Mr. Connor defeated; so we went through postponement after postponement to aid in this community need. After this we felt that direct action could be delayed no longer.

[30] The Birmingham election for mayor was scheduled for March 5th, 1963. Shuttlesworth and King determined to delay their civil rights activities until after the election to avoid Bull Connor's likely efforts to use the protestors for his political advantage in the election. Three pro-segregationist candidates ran and after a run-off election, Albert Boutwell won on April 2nd. The Birmingham Campaign began the next day.

[31] Segregationist Bull Connor was commissioner of public safety in Birmingham for twenty-two years. According to Dr. King, he sought to make Birmingham the most segregated city in America. In 1963, Connor's hostile response to the Birmingham demonstrations helped to bring the America's focus on the civil rights struggle. During his leadership, the city earned the moniker

of "Bombingham" due to the seventeen bombings of black homes and churches. See note 14 above.

II.
C. The Purpose of Direct Action Is to Create Constructive Nonviolent Tension Leading to Negotiation.
1. Constructive, Nonviolent Tension Is Necessary for Growth.

You may well ask, Why direct action? Why sit-ins, [32] marches, etc.? Isn't negotiation a better path?" You are exactly right in your call for negotiation. Indeed, this is the purpose of direct action. Nonviolent direct action seeks to create such a crisis and establish such creative tension that a community that has constantly refused to negotiate is forced to confront the issue. It seeks so to dramatize the issue that it can no longer be ignored. I just referred to the creation of tension as a part of the work of the nonviolent resister. This may sound rather shocking. But I must confess that I am not afraid of the word tension. I have earnestly worked and preached against violent tension, but there is a type of constructive nonviolent tension that is necessary for growth. Just as Socrates[33] felt that it was necessary to create a tension in the mind so that individuals could rise from the bondage of myths and half-truths to the unfettered realm of creative analysis and objective appraisal, we must see the need of having nonviolent gadflies to create the kind of tension in society that will help men rise from the dark depths of prejudice and racism to the majestic heights of understanding and brotherhood.

[32] Beginning in 1960, four black students sat down at Woolworth's white-only lunch counter in downtown Greensboro, North Carolina and refused to leave when asked to do so. This eventually led to the formation of the Student Nonviolent Coordinating Committee (SNCC). Within weeks, sit-ins had occurred at over thirty places in seven states.

[33] Socrates (470BC-399BC) was an ancient Greek philosopher who helped create the seminal concepts of Western philosophy. He is primarily known from Plato's writings. Due to his relentless focus on questions of justice, Socrates was tried in an Athenian court and found guilty of corrupting youth. Refusing to flee, he accepted the sentence of death by poisoning, which was accomplished by drinking a cup of hemlock.

2. Direct Action Seeks to End Monologue and Create a Crisis Situation Leading to Dialogue.

So the purpose of the direct action[34] is to create a situation so crisis-packed that it will inevitably open the door to negotiation. We, therefore, concur with you in your call for negotiation. Too long has our beloved Southland been bogged down in the tragic attempt to live in monologue rather than dialogue.

> [34] Direct action is a type of civil rights protest which was developed by Dr. King with the goal to end the racial injustices that were rampant in legalized segregation. It is a form of political protest that is confrontational in nature with activities that can theoretically range from the non-violent variety practiced by Dr. King to the overt violence perpetrated by guerrilla warfare. Dr. King's non-violent direct action employed marches, strikes, sit-ins, demonstrations, and various forms of peaceful civil disobedience against what were believed to be unjust laws.

II.
D. We Have Not Made a Single Gain in Civil Rights Without Determined Legal and Nonviolent Pressure.

One of the basic points in your statement is that our acts are untimely. Some have asked, "Why didn't you give the new administration time to act?" The only answer that I can give to this inquiry is that the new administration must be prodded about as much as the outgoing one before it acts. We will be sadly mistaken if we feel that the election of Mr. Boutwell[35] will bring the millennium to Birmingham. While Mr. Boutwell is much more articulate and gentle than Mr. Connor, they are both segregationists dedicated to the task of maintaining the status quo. The hope I see in Mr. Boutwell is that he will be reasonable enough to see the futility of massive resistance to desegregation. But he will not see this without pressure from the devotees of civil rights. My friends, I must say to you that we have not made a single gain in civil rights without determined legal and nonviolent pressure. History is the long and tragic story of the fact that privileged groups seldom give up their privileges voluntarily. Individuals may see the moral light and voluntarily give up their unjust posture; but as Reinhold Niebuhr[36] has reminded us, groups are more immoral than individuals.

[35] Albert Burton Boutwell (1904 - 1978), a segregationist, won the 1963 Birmingham mayoral election. Boutwell served for one term.

[36] Karl Paul Reinhold Niebuhr (1892 –1971) was a Protestant theologian and prolific author who analyzed the role of the church in society. Dr. King was deeply influenced by Niebuhr as is seen in a letter from Wayne H. Cowan, the Editor of *Christianity and Crisis* on April 13, 1970 that relates, "I may have told this to Christopher and he may have already repeated it to you. But in case he didn't, let me tell you that Andy Young told me recently that in the quiet hours when he and Martin King would sit and talk that Martin always said he was much more influenced by you and Paul Tillich than by Gandhi and that the nonviolent technique was merely a Niebuhrian stratagem of power. Enough said!"

Niebuhr wrote *Moral Man and Immoral Society* during the Great Depression. Niebuhr argues for the necessity of politics in the quest for social justice because of the reality of human sinfulness seen in the selfishness of both individuals and groups. From his perspective, reason alone cannot conquer social injustice, "since reason is always the servant of interest in a social situation" (pp. xiv-xv). In this way he finds liberal Christian theology misguided in its insistence on human rationality's ability to enable mankind to become truly moral beings.

Accordingly, he establishes a moral divide between individuals and groups and their respective efforts at morality. In fact, the unavoidable experience of humanity is the driving self-interest of the group. Niebuhr's analysis led him to assert that individuals are morally capable of respecting the interests of others and behaving wisely when they perceive conflicts of interest. For Niebuhr, individuals are capable of altruism. For social groups, however, it is nearly an impossibility to resolve the conflicting concerns of their subordinate constituencies in a selfless and rational manner. Groups absorb only the selfishness of individuals, not their magnanimity: Niebuhr's concept referred to by Dr. King here is well expressed in the following, "individuals are morally sensible in their ability to consider the interests of others and to act on their behalf. Individuals can be unselfish. However, in a society or a group of individuals, it is difficult to handle the interest of the group by means of the human rational faculty because groups are only the collection of individuals' selfish impulses, not of their unselfish consideration for others. This collective egoism of individuals becomes more powerful. In every human group there is less reason to guide and to check impulse, less capacity for self-transcendence, less ability to comprehend the needs of others therefore more unrestrained egoism than the individuals, who compose the group, reveal in their personal relationships. Therefore, all social co-operation on a larger scale than the most intimate social group requires a measure of coercion." (pp. xi-xii). Niebuhr writes, "All social co-operation on a larger scale than the most intimate social group requires a measure of coercion" (p. 3). "Every group, as every individual, has expansive desires which are rooted in the instinct of survival and soon extend beyond it. The will-to-live becomes the will-to-power" (p. 18). "Thus society is in a perpetual state of war" (p. 19). His solution is a community in which "...there will be enough justice, and in which coercion will be sufficiently non-violent to prevent [its] common enterprise from issuing into complete disaster" (p. 22). Helpful studies include:

Reinhold Niebuhr, *Moral Man and Immoral Society.* New York: Charles Scribner's Sons, 1932.

Robert McAfee Brown, ed. and intro. *The Essential Reinhold Niebuhr: Selected Essays and Address.* New Haven, CT and London: Yale University Press, 1986.

Charles C. Brown. *Niebuhr and His Age: Reinhold Niebuhr's Prophetic Role in the Twentieth Century.* Philadelphia: Trinity Press International, 1992.

David F. Ford, ed. *The Modern Theologians: An introduction to Christian theology in the twentieth century.* Vol.II. Oxford and Cambridge, MA: Basil Blackwell Ltd., 1989.

II.

E. Freedom Is Never Voluntarily Given by the Oppressor; It Must Be Demanded by the Oppressed. When "Wait" Really Means "Never," We Must See, "Justice Delayed Is Justice Denied."

We know through painful experience that freedom is never voluntarily given by the oppressor; it must be demanded by the oppressed. Frankly I have never yet engaged in a direct action movement that was "well timed," according to the timetable of those who have not suffered unduly from the disease of segregation. For years now I have heard the word "Wait!" It rings in the ear of every Negro with a piercing familiarity. This "wait" has almost always meant "never." It has been a tranquilizing thalidomide, relieving the emotional stress for a moment, only to give birth to an ill-formed infant of frustration. We must come to see with the distinguished jurist of yesterday that "justice too long delayed is justice denied."[37]

[37] This quote has been attributed to Thurgood Marshall, Oliver Wendell Holmes and most often to William Gladstone (1809-1898), British statesman and Prime Minister of England (1868-1894). Sources for this quote used by Dr. King may come from various writings:

> William Penn in 1693 wrote in Fruits of Solitude 69 (11th ed. 1906), "Our Law says well, 'To delay justice, is injustice.'"
>
> Penn seems to have been referring to the *Magna Carta* (1215) Cl.40 states, "To no one will We sell, to no one will We deny or delay, right or justice".
>
> A French author, Jean de la Bruyère (1645 – 1696), an essayist and moralist, wrote: "When it is our duty to do an act of justice, it should be done promptly. To delay is injustice."
>
> An early example in an American legal context declares, "Justice delayed is justice denied" in Gohman v. City of St. Bernard, 111 Ohio St. 726, 737 (1924). See http://lawlibrary.ucdavis.edu/LAWLIB/aug95/0529.html.

II.

F. The Sad History of Segregation Creates Legitimate Impatience for Constitutional and God-given Rights.

1. After 340 years of unspeakable and unjust suffering there is a legitimate and unavoidable impatience.

We have waited for more than three hundred and forty years for our constitutional and God-given rights. The nations of Asia and Africa[38] are moving with jet-like speed toward the goal of political independence, and we still creep at horse and buggy pace toward the gaining of a cup of coffee at a lunch counter.

I guess it is easy for those who have never felt the stinging darts of segregation to say wait. But when you have seen vicious mobs lynch your mothers and fathers at will and drown your sisters and brothers at whim; when you have seen hate filled policemen curse, kick, brutalize, and even kill your black brothers and sisters with impunity; when you see the vast majority of your twenty million Negro brothers smothering in an air-tight cage of poverty in the midst of an affluent society; when you suddenly find your tongue twisted and your speech stammering as you seek to explain to your six-year-old daughter why she can't go to the public amusement park that has just been advertised on television, and see tears welling up in her little eyes when she is told that Funtown is closed to colored children, and see the depressing clouds of inferiority begin to form in her little mental sky, and see her begin to distort her little personality by unconsciously developing a bitterness toward white people; when you have to concoct an answer for a five-year-old son asking in agonizing pathos: "Daddy, why do white people treat colored people so mean?" [39]; when you take a cross-country drive and find it necessary to sleep night after night in the uncomfortable corners of your automobile because no motel will accept you; when you are humiliated day in and day out by nagging signs reading "white" men and "colored"; when your first name becomes "nigger" and your middle name becomes "boy" (however old you are) and your last name becomes "John," and when your wife and mother are never given the respected title "Mrs."; when you are harried by day and haunted by night by the fact that you are a Negro, living constantly at tip-toe stance never quite knowing what to expect next, and plagued with inner fears and outer resentments; when you are forever fighting a degenerating sense of "nobodiness" [40] -- then you will understand why we find it difficult to wait. There comes a time when the cup of endurance runs over, and men are no longer willing to be plunged into an abyss of injustice where they experience the bleakness of corroding despair. I hope, sirs, you can understand our legitimate and unavoidable impatience.

[38] During the Cold War between the United States and the Soviet Union following World War II, many former colonies of Western nations in Africa and Asia pursued and won their independence. While being a colony and experiencing segregation are certainly different in many ways, their common aspiration for freedom and autonomy from external control create a similar concern for civil rights.

[39] A relevant example of this struggle is the story of Emmitt Cornelius, the first African American to earn a Ph.D. ('05) from Westminster Theological Seminary in Philadelphia, Pennsylvania, "Racial Harmony at Westminster" (posted on wts.edu, February 7, 2011. 011):

> I spent most of my childhood and teenage years surrounded by the harsh realities of Jim Crowism and de facto segregation in the South.

I still remember vividly my experiences at all white Boyd Elementary School in the early days of "desegregation" in Jackson, Mississippi. I have never forgotten the hurtful comments (and look) of one elderly white female teacher. Her harsh words and disgruntled demeanor communicated to me that my arrival was unwelcomed and that "forced" busing of black children to white neighborhood schools would never change how whites perceived or treated blacks.

Unfortunately, this was only one of many experiences in the "deep South" that led me to conclude that I did not belong, nor would I ever be accepted, in mainstream America because of the stigma associated with being black. At some point, I stopped believing that racial equality and racial harmony were real possibilities in the world I knew as an African American. As I saw it, slavery and the Jim Crow era had cast too long of a shadow over our nation giving me little hope that the plight of African Americans would ever change.

My introduction to Christ and His church, however, challenged me to reconsider that assessment. Redemption into Christ's covenant community opened up for me a full-blown, biblical vision of how people of different races could live and serve together in racial harmony as witnesses to the transforming and reconciling power of the gospel. As a personal and immensely practical testimony of this, I was blessed as a former African American student at Westminster to have my entire tuition underwritten by a descendant of a former slaveholding family in Mississippi! Imagine. God, in His grace, bringing together offspring of a former slave and a former slaveholder in order to magnify the unrivaled power of His gospel to overcome the evil legacy of racism!

[40] At the core of the Judeo-Christian understanding of human nature is that mankind is made in the image of God, thus human beings

cannot be characterized by the epithet of "nobodiness". This is the climax of the creation account in in Genesis 1:26-28, "Then God said, 'Let us make man in our image, in our likeness, and let them rule over the fish of the sea and the birds of the air, over the livestock, over all the earth, and over all the creatures that move along the ground.' So God created man in his own image, in the image of God he created him; male and female he created them. God blessed them and said to them, 'Be fruitful and increase in number; fill the earth and subdue it. Rule over the fish of the sea and the birds of the air and over every living creature that moves on the ground." This is the heart of why all human beings are "somebodies". In III. G. 1. Dr. King writes, "...so drained of self-respect and a sense of "somebodiness" that they have adjusted to segregation."

2. A Paradox: To Advocate Breaking Some Laws and to Obey Others? "An Unjust Law Is No Law at All."

You express a great deal of anxiety over our willingness to break laws. This is certainly a legitimate concern. Since we so diligently urge people to obey the Supreme Court's decision of 1954 outlawing segregation in the public schools[41], it is rather strange and paradoxical to find us consciously breaking laws. One may well ask: "How can you advocate breaking some laws and obeying others?" The answer is found in the fact that there are two types of laws: There are just laws and there are unjust laws. I would be the first to advocate obeying just laws. One has not only a legal but moral responsibility to obey just laws. Conversely, one has a moral responsibility to disobey unjust laws. I would agree with Saint Augustine that "An unjust law is no law at all." [42]

[41] The beginnings of the Civil Rights movement can be traced in part to the Supreme Court decision, Brown v. Board of Education of Topeka, 347 U.S. 483 (1954). This civil rights victory was achieved under the leadership of the NAACP. Overturning Plessy v. Ferguson (1896), the unanimous Warren Court declared separate public schools for black and white students to be inherently unequal and a violation of the Equal Protection Clause of the Fourteenth Amendment.

[42] Aurelius Augustine; St. Augustine of Hippo (354–430AD) was a Christian theologian, and Catholic bishop in North Africa. Although born a Catholic, Augustine left the faith of his mother to become a Manichaean, a religion that taught that there were two

eternal gods always in conflict with one another, since one was good and the other was evil. He studied rhetoric and taught in various cities in the Roman Empire. Through a dramatic experience of hearing a voice calling him to "take up and read" ("Tolle lege."), he turned to the Bible and was converted to the Christian faith. The text he read as he opened the Bible was Romans 13:14, "Rather, clothe yourselves with the Lord Jesus Christ, and do not think about how to gratify the desires of the sinful nature." Leaving behind his concubine and their child, Augustine converted to Christianity and became a priest, although he took care to nurture his son's growth and spiritual development. In 396 he was appointed the bishop of Hippo. His extensive biblical interpretation, theological and philosophical writings have never ceased to aid the development of Christian thought through the centuries. The quotation that Dr. King cites here, "An unjust law is no law at all", comes from Augustine's *On Free Choice Of The Will*, Book 1, section 5.

III. The Ethical Theory and Issues in Determining Whether a Law Is Just Or Unjust.
A. How Does One Determine Whether a Law Is Just Or Unjust?
1. A Just Law Is a Man-Made Code That Squares with the Moral Law or the Law of God.

Now what is the difference between the two? How does one determine when a law is just or unjust? A just law is a man-made code that squares with the moral law or the law of God. An unjust law is a code that is out of harmony with the moral law. To put it in the terms of Saint Thomas Aquinas, an unjust law is a human law that is not rooted in eternal and natural law. Any law that uplifts human personality is just. Any law that degrades human personality is unjust. [43] All segregation statutes are unjust because segregation distorts the soul and damages the personality. It gives the segregator a false sense of superiority and the segregated a false sense of inferiority. To use the words of Martin Buber, the great Jewish philosopher, segregation substitutes an "I-it" relationship for an "I-thou" relationship, and ends up relegating persons to the status of things. [44] So segregation is not only politically, economically, and sociologically unsound, but it is morally wrong and sinful. Paul Tillich has said that sin is separation. [45] Isn't segregation an existential expression of man's tragic separation, an expression of his awful estrangement, his terrible sinfulness? So I can urge men to obey the 1954 decision of the Supreme Court because it is morally right, and I can urge them to disobey segregation ordinances because they are morally wrong. [46]

[43] St. Thomas Aquinas (1225-1274) was one of the medieval era's leading philosophers and theologians. He is the dominant theologian of the Roman Catholic Church. Aquinas sought to demonstrate the unity between faith and reason, attempting to synthesize historic Christianity with the philosophy of Aristotle. Aquinas taught that natural reason enables the distinction between good and evil due to the impact of divine light of eternal law on human thought. Dr. King's citation of Aquinas is not exact. The phrase, *"Lex iniusta non est lex"*, "an unjust law is not a law" is often attributed to Aquinas, but he never used this exact phase. However one can discover congruent expressions. In Qu. 96, art. 4, corpus. p. 324 (Aquinas, 1993), one reads, "Every human law has just so much of the nature of law, as it is derived from the law of nature. But if at any point it deflects from the law of nature, it is no longer a law but a perversion of law"; and "[unjust laws] are acts of violence rather than laws; because...a law that is not just seems to be no law at all."

Some Catholic ethicists see a difference here between Dr. King and Thomas Aquinas. Charles E. Rice writes, "Martin Luther King: 'One has not only a legal but a moral responsibility to obey just laws. Conversely, one has a moral responsibility to disobey unjust laws. I would agree with St. Augustine that, "an unjust law is no law at all...." To put it in the terms of St. Thomas Aquinas: 'An unjust law is a human law that is not rooted in eternal law and natural law.' *Letter from Birmingham Jail.* Aquinas differs from King in that King says you are obliged to disobey an unjust law. Aquinas says you may be obliged to obey an unjust law." (Lecture 5: Natural Law: For Good Laws , Against Unjust Laws" from course syllabus *Natural Law: What It Is and Why We Need It*, home.comcast.net/~icuweb/ c01005.htm International Catholic University, 10.5).
Rice continues:

Aquinas' definition of law is "an ordinance of reason for the common good, made by him who has care of the community, and promulgated." This definition applies to all four types of law enumerated by Aquinas: Eternal law, Divine law, Natural law and Human law. ... The purpose of law is to promote the common good. ... All law enforces a morality of one sort or another. The issue is not whether the law should enforce morality but which morality it should enforce. ...Aquinas teaches that human law should promote virtue in its effort to promote the common good. Madison and other founders believed that the U.S. Constitution is suited only to a virtuous, moral people. Aquinas says "there is no virtue whose acts cannot be prescribed by the law." But he says, "Human law does not forbid all vicious acts *nor* does it prescribe all acts of virtue." S.T., I, II, Q. 96, art.3; 50 Q., p. 96-97. …Aquinas affirms that just human laws are "binding in conscience." But a law that "deflects from the law of nature" is unjust and "is no longer a law but a perversion of law." …Types of unjust laws:

• *Laws contrary to human good:* beyond authority of lawgiver, oppressive, seriously unequal. No duty to obey unless disobedience would cause scandal or disturbance, i.e., a greater evil.

• *Laws contrary to divine good.* Would compel you to violate divine law. Must disobey.

[44] Martin Buber's *I and Thou* was originally published in 1923 as *Ich und Du* and in English as Martin Buber, *I and Thou,* translated by Ronald Gregor Smith (New York: Charles Scribner's Sons, 1958). Buber's thesis presents an existential philosophy of interpersonal dialogue. He argues that such dialogue can define the nature of human existence. Buber's major theme is that reality can be explained through the manner in which humans engage one another, the world and God. "I-Thou" depicts a relationship of mutual respect between two beings, an authentic existence of interaction with one another without any objectification of the another. The "I-it" relationship stands in opposition to the "I-Thou". "I-It" describes a relationship between a subject the "I", and an object, the "It". As a result, the "I" experiences others beings as things, which leads to dehumanization and the potential tragic expressions of the inhumanity of man to man. The ultimate "I-Thou" relationship is with God, while a measure of this "I-Thou" experience can be had with the world considered as a whole.

[45] Paul Tillich was one of the twentieth century's leading theologians. He taught in various German universities and arrived in the United States in 1933. He was Professor of Philosophical Theology at Union Theological Seminary in New York City and then as University Professor at Harvard University. He wrote several books. The following passage is the likely source of the point that Dr. King makes here. It is taken from Tillich's *The Shaking of the Foundations,* (New York : Charles Scribner's Sons, 1955), Chapter 19: You Are Accepted:

> I should like to suggest another word to you,
> not as a substitute for the word "sin", but as a

useful clue in the interpretation of the word "sin", "separation". Separation is an aspect of the experience of everyone. Perhaps the word "sin" has the same root as the word "asunder". In any case, *sin is separation*. To be in the state of sin is to be in the state of separation. And separation is threefold: there is separation among individual lives, separation of a man from himself, and separation of all men from the Ground of Being. This three-fold separation constitutes the state of everything that exists; it is a universal fact; it is the fate of every life. And it is our human fate in a very special sense. For *we* as men know that we are separated. We not only suffer with all other creatures because of the self-destructive consequences of our separation, but also know *why* we suffer. We know that we are estranged from something to which we really belong, and with which we *should* be united. We know that the fate of separation is not merely a natural event like a flash of sudden lightning, but that it is an experience in which we actively participate, in which our whole personality is involved, and that, as fate, it is also *guilt*. Separation which is fate *and* guilt constitutes the meaning of the word "sin". It is *this* which is the state of our entire existence, from its very beginning to its very end. Such separation is prepared in the mother's womb, and before that time, in every preceding generation. It is manifest in the special actions of our conscious life. It reaches beyond our graves into all the succeeding generations. It is our existence itself. *Existence is separation!* Before sin is an act, it is a state.

[46] The ethics of civil disobedience made an impact on Dr. King from his early studies. In "My Pilgrimage to Nonviolence" he writes, "So when I went to Atlanta's Morehouse College as a freshman in 1944 my concern for racial and economic justice was already substantial. During my student days at Morehouse I read Thoreau's Essay on Civil Disobedience for the first time. Fascinated by the idea of refusing to cooperate with an evil system, I was so deeply moved

> that I reread the work several times. This was my first intellectual contact with the theory of nonviolent resistance." *Papers*, IV, p. 474.

2. An Unjust Law Is a Code a Majority Compels a Minority to Obey But Does Not Make Binding on Itself.

Let us turn to a more concrete example of just and unjust laws. An unjust law is a code that a majority inflicts on a minority that is not binding on itself. This is difference made legal. On the other hand a just law is a code that a majority compels a minority to follow that it is willing to follow itself. This is sameness made legal.

3. A Law Is Unjust If Inflicted on a Minority Denied the Vote, Having No Part in Enacting the Law.

Let me give another explanation. An unjust law is a code inflicted upon a minority which that minority had no part in enacting or creating because they did not have the unhampered right to vote. Who can say that the legislature of Alabama which set up the segregation laws was democratically elected? Throughout the state of Alabama all types of conniving methods are used to prevent Negroes from becoming registered voters and there are some counties without a single Negro registered to vote despite the fact that the Negro constitutes a majority of the population. Can any law set up in such a state be considered democratically structured?

4. Sometimes a Law Is Just on Its Face and Unjust in Its Application.

These are just a few examples of unjust and just laws. There are some instances when a law is just on its face but unjust in its application. For instance, I was arrested Friday on a charge of parading without a permit. Now there is nothing wrong with an ordinance which requires a permit for a parade, but when the ordinance is used to preserve segregation and to deny citizens the First Amendment privilege of peaceful assembly and peaceful protest, then it becomes unjust. [47]

> [47] The First Amendment in the US Constitution is the first of the ten amendments added to the Constitution by the Framers and is called the Bill of Rights. It reads, "Amendment I. Congress shall make no law respecting an establishment of religion, or prohibiting the free

> exercise thereof; or abridging the freedom of speech, or of the press; or the right of the people peaceably to assemble, and to petition the government for a redress of grievances."

5. Key Distinction: Anarchy Is Defying Just Law, Civil Disobedience Is Breaking Unjust Law in Conscience.

I hope you can see the distinction I am trying to point out. In no sense do I advocate evading or defying the law as the rabid segregationist would do. This would lead to anarchy. One who breaks an unjust law must do it openly, lovingly (not hatefully as the white mothers did in New Orleans when they were seen on television screaming "nigger, nigger, nigger") and with a willingness to accept the penalty. I submit that an individual who breaks a law that conscience tells him is unjust, and willingly accepts the penalty by staying in jail to arouse the conscience of the community over its injustice, is in reality expressing the very highest respect for law.

III.
B. Civil Disobedience Against Unjust Laws Is Justified by Biblical and Historical Examples.

Of course there is nothing new about this kind of civil disobedience. [48] It was seen sublimely in the refusal of Shadrach, Meshach, and Abednego to obey the laws of Nebuchadnezzar because a higher moral law was involved. [49] It was practiced superbly by the early Christians who were willing to face hungry lions and the excruciating pain of chopping blocks, before submitting to certain unjust laws of the Roman Empire. [50] To a degree academic freedom is a reality today because Socrates practiced civil disobedience. [51] [52]

> [48] Civil disobedience is the open refusal to obey a government or authority without the use of violence. Henry David Thoreau's 1849 essay, "Resistance to Civil Government" developed a modern expression of the concept of nonviolent resistance and civil disobedience. This work impacted the thinking of Mahatma Gandhi and Dr. King. Yet civil disobedience is an ancient theme that is raised by Scripture as a necessary and inescapable duty under certain circumstances as man seeks to serve and fear God in a fallen and unjust world. For a discussion of various perspectives on the proper understanding of biblical teaching on this matter see

John Jefferson Davis, *Evangelical Ethics: Issues Facing the Church Today* (Phillipsburg: P&R, 1985), pp. 208-226; J. Douma, *The Ten Commandments: Manual for the Christian Life*, trans. Nelson D. Kloosterman (Phillipsburg: P&R, 1996), pp. 175-206; Phillip E. Hughes, *Christian Ethics in Secular Society* (Grand Rapids: Baker, 1983), pp.183-212; John Murray, *Principles of Conduct* (London: Tyndale Press, 1957), pp. 229-242.

[49] This Old Testament story of courageous civil disobedience is found in Daniel chapter 3. Verses 8-14, 16-18 state, "At this time some astrologers came forward and denounced the Jews. They said to King Nebuchadnezzar, 'O king, live forever! You have issued a decree, O king, that everyone who hears the sound of the horn, flute, zither, lyre, harp, pipes and all kinds of music must fall down and worship the image of gold, and that whoever does not fall down and worship will be thrown into a blazing furnace. But there are some Jews whom you have set over the affairs of the province of Babylon—Shadrach, Meshach and Abednego—who pay no attention to you, O king. They neither serve your gods nor worship the image of gold you have set up.' Furious with rage, Nebuchadnezzar summoned Shadrach, Meshach and Abednego. So these men were brought before the king, and Nebuchadnezzar said to them, 'Is it true, Shadrach, Meshach and Abednego, that you do not serve my god or worship the image of gold I have set up?' … Shadrach, Meshach and Abednego replied to the king, 'O Nebuchadnezzar, we do not need to defend ourselves before you in this matter. If we are thrown into the blazing furnace, the God we serve is able to save us from it, and he will rescue us from your hand, O king. But even if he does not, we want you to know, O king that we will not serve your gods or worship the image of gold you have set up.'"

[50] Classic summaries of the courage of the ancient Christian Church to withstand the persecution and tyranny of the Roman Empire are Eusebius of Caesarea's (c.265-c.339AD) *Historia Ecclesiastica* or *Church History* and John Foxe's (1516-1587) *Actes and Monumentes* (first published in 1563) or more popularly known as *Foxe's Book of Martyrs*. Both of these have been reprinted in many versions and are readily available.

[51] See note 33 above.

[52] In the final version, Dr. King adds, "In our own nation, the Boston Tea Party represented a massive act of civil disobedience." For the earliest accounts of this historical event that helped to create the dynamics that led to the American Revolution see www.boston-tea-party.org/accounts.html. Below is the *Boston Gazette* account dated December 20, 1773.

On Tuesday last the body of the people of this and all the adjacent towns, and others from the distance of twenty miles, assembled at the old south meeting-house, to inquire the reason of the delay in sending the ship Dartmouth, with the East-India Tea back to London; and having found that the owner had not taken the necessary steps for that purpose, they enjoin'd him at his peril to demand of the collector of the customs a clearance for the ship, and appointed a committee of ten to see it perform'd; after which they adjourn'd to the Thursday following ten o'clock. They then met and being inform'd by Mr. Rotch, that a clearance was refus'd him, they enjoye'd him immediately to enter a protest and apply to the governor for a pass port by the castle, and adjourn'd again till three o'clock for the same day. At which time they again met and after waiting till near sunset Mr. Rotch came in and inform'd them that he had accordingly enter'd his protest and waited on the governor for a pass, but his excellency told him he could not consistent with his duty grant it until his vessel was qualified. The people finding all their efforts to preserve the property of the East India Company and return it safely to London, frustrated by the sea consignees, the collector of the customs and the governor of the province, DISSOLVED their meeting.--But, BEHOLD what followed! A number of brave & resolute men, determined to do all in their power to save their country from the ruin which their enemies had plotted, in less than four hours, emptied every chest of tea on board the three ships commanded by the captains Hall, Bruce, and Coffin, amounting to 342 chests, into the sea!! without the least damage done to the ships or any other property. The matters and owners are well pleas'd that their ships are thus clear'd; and the people are almost universally congratulating each other on this happy event....

Capt. Loring in a Brig from London for his Place, having 58 Chests of the detested Tea on board, was cast ashore on the Back of Cape-Cod last Friday se'nnight: 'Tis expected the Cape Indians will give us a good Account of the Tea against our next.

Extract of a Letter from Philadelphia, dated December 11, 1773.

--"Your Resolutions of 29th ult. were publickly read at our Coffee-House last Thursday, to a large Company of our first Merchants, who gave three Cheers by Way of Approbation."

We hear from Philadelphia, that Capt. Ayres, in a Ship chartered by the East India Company, to bring their Teas to that Place, had arrived at the Cape of Deleware (Mr. Gilbert Barclay, one of the Consignees, being Passenger on board) but that the Pilots had refused to bring her up the River; and Letters being sent to the Captain & Consignee, inclosing their Resolves respecting each of them, that if they presumed to come thither, it would be at their Peril, and the inevitable Destruction of both Vessel and Cargo; in Consequence of which intelligence, it was said they had gone off, but whether to the Place from whence they cause, or same other Port, was uncertain; though this might be depended on, that they would not be permitted to land the Tea in any Part of that Province.

We are positively informed that the patriotic inhabitants of Lexington, at a late meeting, unanimously resolved against the use of Bohea Tea of all sorts, Dutch or English importation; and to manifest the sincerity of their resolution, they bro't together every ounce contained in the town, and committed it to one common bonfire.

We are also informed, Charlestown is in motion to follow their illustrious example. Quere. Would it not materially affect the bringing this detestable herb into disuse, if every town would enjoin their Selectmen to deny licences to all houses of entertainment who were known to afford tea to their guests?

Our reason for suggesting this, is the difficulty these people are under to avoid dishing out this poison, without such a provision in their favour.

III.
C. The Legal Can Be Unjust and the Illegal Can Be Just.

We can never forget that everything Hitler did in Germany was "legal"[53] and everything the Hungarian freedom fighters did in Hungary was "illegal." [54] It was "illegal" to aid and comfort a Jew in Hitler's Germany. But I am sure that, if I had lived in Germany during that time, I would have aided and comforted my Jewish brothers even though it was illegal. If I lived in a communist country today where certain principles dear to the Christian faith are suppressed, I believe I would openly advocate disobeying these anti-religious laws. [55]

[53] Adolf Hitler's success in bringing the German government under his control meant that every law that was passed to further his desire to subjugate Europe and to destroy the Jews was entirely legal even if immoral. Hitler's anti-Semitism was enunciated in 1924 with chilling clarity in *Mein Kampf* that began to be put into horrific practice only a little over a decade later:

Peoples who can sneak their way into the rest of mankind like drones, to make other men work for them under all sorts of pretexts, can form states even without any definitely delimited living space of their own. This applies first and foremost to a people under whose parasitism the whole of honest humanity is suffering, today more than ever: The Jews.

The Jewish state was never spatially limited in itself, but universally unlimited as to space, though restricted in the sense of embracing but one race. Consequently, this people has always formed a state within states. It is one of the most ingenious tricks that was ever devised, to make this state sail under the flag of 'religion,' thus assuring it of the tolerance which the Aryan is always ready to accord a religious creed. For actually the Mosaic religion is nothing other than a doctrine for the preservation of the Jewish race. It therefore embraces almost all sociological, political, and economic fields of knowledge which can have any bearing on this function (pp. 150-151).

The foremost connoisseurs of this truth regarding the possibilities in the use of falsehood and slander have always been the Jews; for after all, their whole existence is based on one single great lie, to wit, that they are a religious community while actually they are a race— and what a race! One of the greatest minds of humanity has nailed them forever as such in an eternally correct phrase of fundamental truth: he called them 'the great masters of the lie.' And anyone who does not recognize this or does not want to believe it will never in this world be able to help the truth to victory. (p. 232).

…the Jew never thinks of leaving a territory that he has occupied, but remains where he is, and he sits so fast that even by force it is very hard to drive him out.…The Jew's life as a parasite in the body of other nations and states explains a characteristic which once caused Schopenhauer, as has already been mentioned, to call him the 'great master in lying.' Existence impels the Jew to lie, and to lie perpetually just as it compels the inhabitants of the northern countries to wear warm clothing (p. 305). Adolf Hitler, *Mein Kampf*, Trans., Ralph Manheim (Boston: Houghton Mifflin Co., 1943).

Hitler's fully legal application of force against the Jews illustrates the difference between "positive law" and "natural law" as taught in Roman Catholic thought emerging from the writings of Thomas Aquinas. Charles Rice, *op. cit.* in note 42 above, says,

> There are only two games in town on the issue of the whether there are any moral limits to law: legal positivism or some form of natural law. … Kelsen and other legal positivists say a law that is enacted according to prescribed procedures is a valid law e.g., the Nazi and Soviet regimes. The Supreme Court's approach to personhood illustrates legal positivism in action. Personhood is the prerequisite for the constitutional right to life. The N.Y. Court of Appeals, in the 1972 Byrn case, said the legislature can define some innocent human beings as nonpersons. *Roe v. Wade* took the same approach. So did *Dred Scott* and the Nazi depersonalization of the Jews. Legal positivism allows no room for disobedience of a law enacted by the prescribed procedures. "[A]ll attempts at . . . resistance to the [Nazi] regime were necessarily grounded on natural law ideas or on divine law, for legal positivism as such could offer no foundation."

[54] In 1945, as World War II ended, the Soviet Union liberated Hungary from the Nazis only to subjugate them under the iron fist of Khrushchev, Stalin's successor. The Hungarian Revolution of 1956 was a spontaneous nationwide revolt against the Soviet Communist controlled government of the People's Republic of Hungary. It began on the 23rd of October and ended November 10, 1956. Stalin had died only a few years earlier, and Khrushchev had assumed command of the Soviet Union, and there seemed to be a spirit of

liberalization in the air marked by Khrushchev's criticism of Stalin. The revolt started as a student demonstration with thousands marching through central Budapest to the Parliament building. Shots were fired against the student protestors, and soon violence erupted throughout the city.

As the revolution swept through the nation, the government fell. At first, the Politburo seemed open to a negotiated withdrawal of Soviet forces. But on November 4th, the Soviet armed forces invaded Hungary. Resistance lasted until November10th during which time 2,500 Hungarians and hundreds of Soviet troops were killed. Some 200,000 Hungarians fled leaving others to face arrest, execution and repression. The military suppression of the revolt was successful, but it deeply troubled many in the West including some who had espoused Marxist ideology. Thus the iron curtain fell forcefully over Hungary, but in doing so, it also left a fatal fissure in the Soviet Union's prestige on the world stage that would eventually be exploited by the West leading ultimately to the end of Soviet Communist domination of Eastern Europe.

[55] Anatolii Lunarchskii, the Soviet Minister of Education in 1928 said in a seemingly prophetic comment: "Religion is like a nail, the harder you hit it, the deeper it goes into the wood." The US commitment to religious liberty is well stated in President Franklin D. Roosevelt's address to the U.S. Congress on January 6, 1941:

> In the future days which we seek to make secure, we look forward to a world founded upon four essential human freedoms. The first is freedom of speech and expression—everywhere in the world. The second is freedom of every person to worship God in his own way—everywhere in the world. The third is freedom from want—which, translated into world terms, means economic undertakings which will secure to every nation a healthy peacetime life for its inhabitants— everywhere in the world. The fourth is freedom from fear—which, translated into world terms, means a worldwide reduction of armaments to such a point and in such a thorough fashion that no nation will be in a position to commit an act of physical aggression against any neighbor— anywhere in the world. . . . Freedom means the supremacy of human rights everywhere.

In this context, another event with vast significance for religious liberty worldwide was the promulgation in 1965 of the *Declaration of Religious Freedom* or *Dignitatis Humanae* by the Second Vatican Council. Its significance lies in the immense worldwide influence of the Roman Catholic tradition, not only in past history, but in contemporary international affairs as well. Its powerful language clarifies once and for all that the Roman Catholic Church rejects the persecution of minority faiths, and that it is committed to universal religious liberty and the liberty of the conscience. *Dignitatis Humanae* declares:

> A sense of the dignity of the human person has been impressing itself more and more deeply on the consciousness of contemporary man, and the demand is increasingly made that men should act on their own judgment, enjoying and making use of a responsible freedom, not driven by coercion but motivated by a sense of duty. The demand is likewise made that constitutional limits should be set to the powers of government, in order that there may be no encroachment on the rightful freedom of the individual and of associations. This demand for freedom in human society chiefly concerns the quest for the values proper to the human spirit. It concerns, in the first place, the free exercise of religion in society. This Vatican Council takes careful note of these desires in the minds of men. It proposes to declare that they are greatly in accord with truth and justice. This Vatican Council declares that the human person has a right to religious freedom. This freedom means that all men are to be immune from coercion on the part of individuals or of social groups and of any human power, in such ways that in religious matters no one is to be forced to act in a manner contrary to his own conscience, whether privately or publicly, whether alone or in association with others, within due limits. The council further declares that the right to religious freedom has its foundation in the very dignity of the human person as this dignity is known through the revealed word of God and by reason

> itself. This right of the human person to religious freedom is to be recognized in the constitutional law whereby society is governed and thus it is to become a civil right.
>
> See Peter A. Lillback, *Proclaim Liberty...A Broken Bell Rings Freedom to the World* (Bryn Mawr: Providence Forum Press, 2001), pp. 54-56.

III.
D. An Expression of Grave Disappointment with the White Moderate.
1. Seeking Order Rather than Justice, Preferring an Absence of Tension Rather Than a Presence of Justice.

I must make two honest confessions to you, my Christian and Jewish brothers. First, I must confess that over the last few years I have been gravely disappointed with the white moderate. I have almost reached the regrettable conclusion that the Negroes' great stumbling block in the stride toward freedom is not the White Citizen's "Counciler[56] " or the Ku Klux Klanner[57], but the white moderate who is more devoted to "order"[58] than to justice[59]; who prefers a negative peace which is the absence of tension to a positive peace which is the presence of justice; who constantly says "I agree with you in the goal you seek, but I can't agree with your methods of direct action"; who paternalistically feels that he can set the timetable for another man's freedom; who lives by the myth of time and who constantly advises the Negro to wait until a "more convenient season." [60] Shallow understanding from people of good will is more frustrating than absolute misunderstanding from people of ill will. Lukewarm acceptance is much more bewildering than outright rejection. [61]

---

[56] Founded in 1954, the White Citizens Council was often identified as a more civilized edition of the Ku Klux Klan, a sort of "white collar Klan". The White Citizens Council overtly sought to stymie efforts to end segregation. As white supremacists, they acted intentionally as a racist organization but did not explicitly affirm the use of violence or terrorist activities.

[57] Ku Klux Klan (KKK) refers to various organizations in the United States that have asserted white supremacy and racism. Anti-Semitism, anti-Communism and anti-homosexuality have often played a role in their agenda. African Americans in the south

were often victimized by the KKK by overt oppression through intimidation, violence and terrorism. Burning of crosses in victims' yard was a classic KKK ploy of psychological assault upon African-Americans as well as a warning to them to keep in their place in a segregated society.

[58] Order is an important concern of the church, but it is to be coupled with that which is fitting or decent. The Apostle Paul writes in 1 Corinthians 14:40, "But everything should be done in a fitting and orderly way."

[59] One of the classic Old Testament texts on mankind's duty to pursue justice is Micah 6:8, "He has showed you, O man, what is good. And what does the Lord require of you? To act justly and to love mercy and to walk humbly with your God."

[60] This quotation "a more convenient season" is a direct reference to the KJV's Acts 24:25, "And as he reasoned of righteousness, temperance, and judgment to come, Felix trembled, and answered, 'Go thy way for this time; when I have a convenient season, I will call for thee.'" The NIV says, "As Paul discoursed on righteousness, self-control and the judgment to come, Felix was afraid and said, 'That's enough for now! You may leave. When I find it convenient, I will send for you.'"

[61] There is an allusion here to Revelation 3:15-16, Christ's rebuke to the Church in Laodicea: "I know your deeds, that you are neither cold nor hot. I wish you were either one or the other! So, because you are lukewarm—neither hot nor cold—I am about to spit you out of my mouth."

2. Law and Order Exist for the Purpose of Establishing Justice. Nonviolent Direct Action Exposes Injustice.

I had hoped that the white moderate would understand that law and order exist for the purpose of establishing justice, and that when they fail to do this they become dangerously structured dams that block the flow of social progress. I had hoped that the white moderate would understand that the present tension in the South is merely a necessary phase of the transition from an obnoxious negative peace, where the Negro passively accepted his unjust plight, to a substance-filled positive peace, where all men will respect the dignity and worth of human personality. Actually, we who engage in nonviolent direct action are not the creators of tension. We merely bring to the surface the hidden tension that is already alive. We bring it out in the open where it can be seen and dealt with. Like a boil that can never be cured as long as it is covered up but must be opened with all its pus-flowing ugliness to the natural medicines of air and light, injustice must likewise be exposed, with all of the tension its exposing creates, to the light of human conscience and the air of national opinion before it can be cured.

III.
E. It Is Wrong to Urge One to Cease Efforts for Constitutional Rights Because This May Result in Violence.

In your statement you asserted that our actions, even though peaceful, must be condemned because they precipitate violence. But can this assertion be logically made? Isn't this like condemning the robbed man because his possession of money precipitated the evil act of robbery? Isn't this like condemning Socrates because his unswerving commitment to truth and his philosophical delvings precipitated the misguided popular mind to make him drink the hemlock?[62] Isn't this like condemning Jesus because His unique God consciousness[63] and never-ceasing devotion to His will[64] precipitated the evil act of crucifixion?[65] We must come to see, as federal courts have consistently affirmed, that it is immoral to urge an individual to withdraw his efforts to gain his basic constitutional rights because the quest precipitates violence.[66] Society must protect the robbed and punish the robber.

[62] See note 33 above.

[63] Jesus' unique God-consciousness is clearly seen in the Gospels and has been an occasion of substantial theological debate among theologians. These discussions are prompted by texts such as: Mark 10:17-18, "'Why do you call me good' Jesus answered. 'No one is good—except God alone.'" John 8:57-59, "'You are not yet fifty years old,' the Jews said to him, 'and you have seen Abraham!' 'I tell you the truth,' Jesus answered, 'before Abraham was born, I am!' At this, they picked up stones to stone him, but Jesus hid himself, slipping away from the temple grounds." John 14:6-9, "Jesus answered, 'I am the way and the truth and the life. No one comes to the Father except through me. If you really knew me, you would know my Father as well. From now on, you do know him and have seen him.' Philip said, 'Lord show us the Father and that will be enough for us.' Jesus answered: 'Don't you know me, Philip, even after I have been among you such a long time? Anyone who has seen me has seen the Father. How can you say, "Show us the Father?"'"

[64] Gospel texts that are behind Dr. King's statement include: Luke 2:49,

"'Why were you searching for me?' he asked. 'Didn't you know I had to be in my Father's house?'" Matthew 3:13-15, "Then Jesus came from Galilee to the Jordan to be baptized by John. But John tried to deter him, saying, 'I need to be baptized by you, and do you come to me?' Jesus replied, 'Let it be so now; it is proper for us to do this to fulfill all righteousness.' Then John consented." Matthew 6:9-10, "This, then, is how you should pray: 'Our Father in heaven, hallowed be your name, your kingdom come, your will be done on earth as it in heaven.'" John 5:19-20, "Jesus gave them this answer: 'I tell you the truth, the Son can do nothing by himself; he can do only what he sees his Father doing, because whatever the Father does the Son also does. For the Father loves the Son and shows him all he does.'" John 6:38-39, "For I have come down from heaven not to do my will but to do the will of him who sent me. And this is the will of him who sent me, that I shall lose none of all that he has given me, but raise them up at the last day."

[65] John 5:17-18, "Jesus said to them, 'My Father is always at his work to this very day, and I, too, am working.' For this reason the Jews tried all the harder to kill him; not only was he breaking the Sabbath, but he was even calling God his own Father, making himself equal with God." John 19:6-7, "As soon as the Chief priests and their officials saw him, they shouted, 'Crucify!' 'Crucify!' But Pilate answered, 'You take him and crucify him. As for me, I find no basis for a charge against him.' The Jews insisted, 'We have a law, and according to that law he must die, because he claimed to be the Son of God.'"

[66] "Quotable Quotes from Federal Court Judge in University of Wyoming Free Speech Lawsuit", *May 14, 2010* by Adam Kissel summarizes an example of the judicial decisions that Dr. King refers to here.

> ... we have a ringing endorsement of the Bill of Rights from The Honorable William F. Downes, Chief United States District Judge, ...

The Bill of Rights is a document for all seasons. We don't just display it when the weather is fair and put it away when the storm is tempest. To be a free people, we must have the courage to exercise our constitutional rights. To be a prudent people, we have to protect the rights of others, recognizing that that is the best guarantor of our own rights....

Judge Downes also compares the pitiful level of evidence presented by the university against significant evidence of likely violence during the civil rights movement in a case where the speech was allowed to take place anyway…

In March of 1965, Judge Frank Johnson of the United States District Court for the Middle District of Alabama was asked to enjoin the State of Alabama from interfering with the march of civil rights leaders from Selma to Montgomery, Alabama. Judge Johnson's decision in the case of Williams versus Wallace, 240 F.Supp. 100, Middle District of Alabama 1965, was issued just 12 days after what's now known in history as "Bloody Sunday." On Bloody Sunday, March 7, 1965, 600 or so civil rights marchers headed east out of Selma on U.S. Route 80. They got only as far as the notorious Edmond Pettus Bridge, six blocks away, where state and local lawmen, acting under the color of law, attacked them with billy clubs and tear gas and drove them back into Selma.

At a time when the American south was a virtual powder keg of racial hostility and social unrest, arguments were made to Judge Johnson that violence would likely be carried out against the marchers, a fact all too well known to Judge Johnson based on the events of March 7.

Nonetheless, Judge Johnson rejected the State of Alabama's position that threats of violence from those who opposed the exercise of free speech can serve as a sufficient justification to cancel constitutional dictates. Judge Johnson wrote: The State's contention that there is some hostility to this march will not justify its denial. Nor will the threat of violence constitute an excuse for its denial. Id. at page 109, citations omitted.…

This line of reasoning is powerful and controversial. In the article just cited, Adam Kissel argues in support of the federal judge who follows Dr. King's First Amendment reasoning to protects the right of a student at the University of Wyoming to have the controversial Bill Ayers to speak at a student meeting even when the University was in opposition to the Ayers' lecturing on their campus. Dr. King's same First Amendment logic is also appealed to by Father Frank Pavone, National Director of Priests for Life in opposition to the continuing governmental defense of partial birth abortion. Father Pavone writes in his article, "Inciting Violence":

States all over the country are passing bans on the partial-birth abortion procedure. Legislators in Missouri recently voted to override their Governor's veto of such legislation.

The next step on the part of pro-abortion forces was to use the Court system to stop the law from taking effect. (Supporters of abortion know that they cannot get support for their extreme views from the public, so seek help from a handful of judges instead.)

What should really catch our attention, though, is one of the reasons that the Governor of Missouri gave for his veto of the partial-birth abortion ban. The Governor was reported to say that the legislation *would constitute an open invitation to violence against abortion providers.*

Now let me get this straight.

Legislation which prohibits an act of violence against a baby is bad, because it invites people to kill those who kill the baby? I wonder how many other acts of violence should therefore be *permitted* under law so that people won't feel justified in killing those who carry them out. This is upside-down thinking if there ever was such a thing.

Abortion supporters have been using this line for a while. I myself have been accused of inflaming violence simply because I write and preach that abortion is "killing."

Let's go back a few decades in history. When Rev. Martin Luther King, Jr. was exposing racial injustice and mobilizing people to correct it, he received a letter from eight Alabama clergymen. Part of the letter read,

> *"Just as we formerly pointed out that 'hatred and violence have no sanction in our religious and political traditions,' we also point out that such actions as incite to hatred and violence, however technically peaceful those actions may be, have not contributed to the resolution of our local problems.*

Dr. King responded with his famous *Letter from a Birmingham Jail*, in which he wrote,

> *"In your statement you assert that our actions, even though peaceful, must be condemned because they precipitate violence. But is this a logical assertion? Isn't this like condemning a robbed man because his possession of money precipitated the evil act of robbery? Isn't this like condemning Socrates because his unswerving commitment to truth and his philosophical inquiries precipitated the act by the misguided populace in which they made him drink hemlock? Isn't this like condemning Jesus*

> *because his unique God -consciousness and never-ceasing devotion to God's will precipitated the evil act of crucifixion? We must come to see that, as the Federal courts have consistently affirmed, it is wrong to urge an individual to cease his efforts to gain his basic constitutional rights because the quest may precipitate violence. Society must protect the robbed and punish the robber."*

In our day, what actually promotes violence is the pro-choice mentality. When someone kills an abortion provider, he/she is practicing what pro-choicers have preached for decades: that sometimes it is OK to choose to end a life to solve a problem.

III.

F. Human Progress Is not Inevitable; It Comes by the Tireless Efforts of Men As Co-Workers with God.

I had also hoped that the white moderate would reject the myth of time. I received a letter this morning from a white brother in Texas which said: "All Christians know that the colored people will receive equal rights eventually, but is it possible that you are in too great of a religious hurry? It has taken Christianity almost 2,000 years to accomplish what it has. The teachings of Christ take time to come to earth."[67] All that is said here grows out of a tragic misconception of time. It is the strangely irrational notion that there is something in the very flow of time that will inevitably cure all ills. Actually time is neutral. It can be used either destructively or constructively. I am coming to feel that the people of ill will have used time much more effectively than the people of good will. We will have to repent in this generation[68] not merely for the vitriolic words and actions of the bad people, but for the appalling silence of the good people. We must come to see that human progress never rolls in on wheels of inevitability. It comes through the tireless efforts and persistent work of men willing to be co-workers with God,[69] and without this hard work time itself becomes an ally of the forces of social stagnation.

We must use time creatively, and forever realize that the time is always ripe to do right. Now is the time[70] to make real the promise of democracy, and transform our pending national elegy[71] into a creative psalm of brotherhood.[72] Now is the time to lift our national policy from the quicksand of racial injustice to the solid rock[73] of human dignity.[74]

67 The advice of the Texan quoted here by Dr. King concerning the painfully slow but inevitable progress and impact of the teaching of Christianity on human history echoes in the story of Onesimus the runaway slave in Paul's Epistle to Philemon. Philemon had become a believer under Paul's ministry and was being sent back as a slave but also as a Christian brother. Verses 10-17 relate, "I appeal to you for my son Onesimus, who became my son while I was in chains. Formerly he was useless to you, but now he has become useful both to you and to me. I am sending him—who is my very heart—back to you I would have like to keep him with me so that he could take your place in helping me while I am in chains for the gospel But I did not want to do anything without your consent so that any favor you do will be spontaneous and not forced. Perhaps the reason was that you might have him back for good—no longer as a slave but better than a slave, as a dear brother. He is very dear to me but even dearer to you, both as a man and as a brother in the Lord. So if you consider me a partner, welcome him as you would welcome me." This small progress at ending slavery under Paul only became a universal reality in Christian society some 18 centuries later after Wilberforce's efforts in the United Kingdom and after the Civil War in the US.

The slow progress and ongoing struggle of the Christian faith to impact culture in history is poignantly depicted in Henry Wadsworth Longfellow's *Christmas Bells*, based on Luke 2:14, "Glory to God in the highest, and on earth peace, good will toward men." The poem was written in the midst of the Civil War after his own son in the Union Army had died in battle.

> I heard the bells on Christmas Day
> Their old familiar carols play,
> And wild and sweet
> The words repeat
> Of peace on earth, good-will to men!
>
> And thought how, as the day had come,
> The belfries of all Christendom
> Had rolled along
> The unbroken song
> Of peace on earth, good-will to men!
>
> Till, ringing, singing on its way,

The world revolved from night to day,
A voice, a chime

A chant sublime
Of peace on earth, good-will to men!

Then from each black accursed mouth
The cannon thundered in the South,
And with the sound
The carols drowned
Of peace on earth, good-will to men!

It was as if an earthquake rent
The hearth-stones of a continent,
And made forlorn
The households born
Of peace on earth, good-will to men!

And in despair I bowed my head;
"There is no peace on earth," I said;
"For hate is strong,
And mocks the song
Of peace on earth, good-will to men!"

Then pealed the bells more loud and deep:
"God is not dead; nor doth he sleep!
The Wrong shall fail,
The Right prevail,
With peace on earth, good-will to men!"

[68] Dr. King's "We will have to repent in this generation" reflects Jesus' teaching in Matthew 12:39-42; 17:17; Luke 11:29-32, 50-51; as well as that of Peter and Paul in Acts 2:40; Philippians 2:15. Matthew 12:39 -42 says, "He answered, 'A wicked and adulterous generation asks for a miraculous sign! … The men of Nineveh will stand up at the judgment with this generation and condemn it; for they repented at the preaching of Jonah, and now one greater than Jonah is here. The Queen of the South will rise at the judgment with this generation and condemn it; for she came from the ends of the earth to listen to Solomon's wisdom, and now one greater than Solomon is here.'"

[69] Paul teaches that believers are co-workers with God. 1 Corinthians

3:9, "For we are God's fellow workers; you are God's field, God's building." 2 Corinthians 5:20, "We are therefore Christ's ambassadors, as though God were making his appeal through us. We implore you on Christ's behalf: Be reconciled to God." 2 Corinthians 6:1 says, "As God's fellow workers we urge you not to receive God's grace in vain." 1 Thessalonians 3:2 says, "We sent Timothy who is our brother and God's fellow worker in spreading the gospel of Christ, to strengthen and encourage you in your faith." Mark 16:20 also supports this idea, "Then the disciples went out and preached everywhere, and the Lord worked with them and confirmed his word by the signs that accompanied it."

70 2 Corinthians 6:2 emphasizes the immediacy of salvation by declaring "now is the time...." That text reads, "For he says, 'In the taime of my favor I heard you, and in the day of salvation I helped you.' I tell you, now is the time of God's favor, now is the day of salvation."

71 An elegy is a poem that focuses on the death of a person or a group of people and accordingly is lyrical in nature with a sad and somber tone. It seeks to express emotions and perceptions about the deceased and less about facts making it distinct from a narrative poem. Feelings of grief, sorrow and loss are intertwined with honor for the departed as well as interpretations of his/her or their life/lives on earth. An excellent example is Thomas Gray's "Elegy Written in a Country Churchyard" written in the mid-1700s. Gray's poem reflects on the lives of simple and largely unknown people interred in a church's cemetery of a church. So when Dr. King speaks of our "pending national elegy", he is warning his readers that America's epitaph or a poem on the death of our beloved nation is imminent. The success or failures of the struggles in Birmingham were thus foreboding the demise of America if segregation and racial oppression were not effectively addressed by nonviolence and the unity of racial brotherhood.

72 "...a creative psalm of brotherhood" is a reference to Psalm 133:1-3, "How good and pleasant it is when brothers live together in unity! It is like precious oil poured on the head, running down on the beard, running down on Aaron's beard, down upon the collar of his robes. It is as if the dew of Hermon were falling on Mount Zion. For there the Lord bestows his blessing, even life forevermore."

73 Dr. King here makes allusion to Jesus' teaching at the conclusion of the Sermon on the Mount, Matthew 7:24-27, "Therefore everyone who hears these words of mine and puts them into practice is like a wise man who built his house on the rock. The rain came down, the

streams rose, and the winds blew and beat against that house; yet it did not fall, because it had its foundation on the rock. But everyone who hears these words of mine and does not put them into practice is like a foolish man who built his house on sand. The rain came down, the streams rose, and the winds blew and beat against that house, and it fell with a great crash."
[74] See note 39 above.

III.
G. Nonviolent "Extremism" Is the Way of Love and Stands Against Both Complacency and Hatred.
1. Disappointment That Clergymen See Nonviolence as Extremism. It Is Between Complacency & Violence.

You spoke of our activity in Birmingham as extreme. At first I was rather disappointed that fellow clergymen would see my nonviolent efforts as those of the extremist. I started thinking about the fact that I stand in the middle of two opposing forces in the Negro community. One is a force of complacency made up of Negroes who, as a result of long years of oppression, have been so completely drained of self-respect and a sense of "somebodiness" that they have adjusted to segregation, and of a few Negroes in the middle class who, because of a degree of academic and economic security, and because at points they profit by segregation, have unconsciously become insensitive to the problems of the masses. The other force is one of bitterness and hatred and comes perilously close to advocating violence. It is expressed in the various black nationalist groups that are springing up over the nation, the largest and best known being Elijah Muhammad's Muslim movement.[75] This movement is nourished by the contemporary frustration over the continued existence of racial discrimination. It is made up of people who have lost faith in America, who have absolutely repudiated Christianity, and who have concluded that the white man is an incurable "devil."[76]

[75] Elijah Muhammad (born Elijah Robert Poole; October 7, 1897 — February 25, 1975) was the leader of the Black Muslims, but his teachings were learned from the founder of the Nation of Islam, Master Fard Muhammad. "The Prophet," as Master Fard Muhammad was known, created the Temple of Islam in 1930 in Detroit. He sought to teach the truth about the evil of the white man, that blacks must anticipate the coming of Armageddon--the inevitable battle between black and white, that black men should

not be called "Negroes" and that Christianity was not the religion of the blacks, but the religion of the oppressors of the blacks, the whites who were their former slave masters.

After Fard disappeared in 1934, Elijah Muhammad became the Minister of Islam. Mr. Fard was subsequently deified as Allah and his birthday, Feb. 26, is observed throughout the Nation of Islam as Saviour's Day. Elijah Muhammad then became known as the "Messenger of Allah," and considered by Black Muslims as the "Last Messenger of Allah." This claim for Elijah Muhammad clearly placed the Black Muslim movement in direct conflict with historic Islam that identifies Muhammad of the *Qur'an* as the last prophet of Allah.

Elijah Muhammad's religious principles claimed that Islam is the true religion. This was expressed in such teachings as: "doing for oneself" is necessary, the black man is supreme and the white man is "the devil." He kept Black Muslims from participating in the American political process, teaching that what was to be accomplished by the Nation of Islam was to be divinely achieved though natural catastrophes and warring among whites. He was an advocate of independent, black-operated businesses, institutions, and religion. The movement is highly disciplined with strict rules regarding eating, drinking, and behavior. Members are forbidden from eating pork, smoking and drinking. The use of drugs, profanity, and dancing are prohibited. All members are to be well dressed and groomed. Elijah Muhammad taught that blacks were the first human beings, but that a misguided black scientist named Yakub had created a white beast and that whites had consequently been given a limited period of history in which to govern the world, a period, however, that was soon due to conclude. This meant that the time had come for blacks to reassert their initial dominance in history even if violence and open war were required for the triumph of the blacks over the whites. As a means to this end, Elijah Muhammad advanced the goal for an independent nation for African Americans. Elijah Muhammad even claimed that a Mother Plane, a secret space ship with superior beings patrolled the heavens tracking the devil which was also prepared to deliver Black Muslims from the approaching racial Armageddon.

However, Elijah Muhammad contended that his identification of whites as "blue-eyed devils" was neither to hate them nor to teach hatred. He once declared, "They say that I am a preacher of racial hatred but the fact is that the white people don't like the truth, especially if it speaks against them. It is a terrible thing for such people to charge me with teaching race hatred when their feet are on my people's neck and they tell us to our face that they hate black people. Remember now, they even teach you that you must not hate them for hating you."

He was convicted of exhorting his followers to avoid the draft and was sent to Federal prison in Milan, Michigan for nearly four years, where he continued to lead the Nation of Islam from behind bars. The Black Muslim's most famous member, Malcolm X, joined the Nation of Islam in a Massachusetts prison. When he was released from jail in August, 1952, Malcolm X quickly rose to leadership in the Nation of Islam.

By 1963, having converted the boxing champion Muhammad Ali to the faith, Malcolm X became unhappy with Elijah Mohammed's leadership. He believed Mr. Muhammad's religious interpretations that excluded Caucasian Moslems were too restrictive. He also desired the Black Muslims to set aside the policy of non-engagement in civil rights and political affairs. Malcolm X was assassinated in 1965 allegedly by three Black Muslims. Elijah Muhammad died at age 77 in 1975.

The Black Muslim movement in America is distinct from traditional Islam. C. Eric Lincoln explains,

> The Black Muslims are not generally accepted by the orthodox Moslem groups in America. Race is probably not a major factor in this rejection, although there is a marked clannishness among American Moslems of European descent. Some of the earliest Moslem converts in America were black followers of Soufi Abdul-Hamid, a Black American who embraced Islam during his travels in Asia, and black orthodox Moslems remain scattered about the country in small numbers occasionally augmented by the conversion of black celebrities such as Imamu Amiri Baraka (Leroi Jones), and Abdul Jabbar (Lew Alcindor). The rejection of the Black Muslims is more likely traceable to[Elijah] Muhammad's extreme racial views, his emphatic militancy and his unhistoric teachings about the Black Nation. American Moslems do not wish to be identified with such doctrines. (C. Eric Lincoln, Boston: Beacon Press, *The Black Muslims in America*, 1973, pp. 182-83).

While there are areas of overlap between Muslims and Black Muslims, they must ultimately be differentiated.

[76] The teaching of the white man as the "devil" has made its way into the FBI report on Elijah Muhammad. Through the freedom of information act, the FBI report on Elijah Muhammad (File: 105-24822) is available on line at foia.fbi.gov/foiaindex/muhammad.htm. In the report under the section identified as I. Background , one finds,

> The NOI [Nation of Islam] is an all-black nationwide organization headquartered at Muhammad's Temple 2, 7351 South Stony Island Avenue, Chicago, Illinois, under the guidance of ELIJAH MUHAMMAD, self-styled "Messenger of Allah" and alleged divinely appointed leader of the black race in the United States. Its purpose is separation of the black man from the "devil" (white race) through establishment of a black nation. Followers are instructed to obey the laws of the land if they do not conflict with NOI laws and not to carry weapons but are to defend NOI officials, their property, women and themselves if attacked at all costs and are to take weapons away from their attackers and use same on the attacker.

There is further teaching by Elijah Muhammad about the difference between the origins of the American Indian and the Negro in America. But perhaps his strongest assertion is in regard to freedom for the black:

> We, the lost and found members of our Nation, the original black nation of the earth, called Negros—a name given to us by the slave masters, along with their own, which have no divine meaning—need some of this earth on which we can build a home of our own. If we now are free and must go for self, we must have some of this earth to live free on so that we can exercise freedom of action. The freed slave is not to depend on his ex-slave-master for the necessities of life. This is the free slave's responsibility. The

slave must be educated into the knowledge of how to do for self....It is the free man's duty to accept his own responsibilities accompanying freedom. If one were to care for us, taking the responsibility for us, we would become a servant to that one. We are in bondage to whosoever takes our responsibilities to care for us...We love freedom. If we love freedom for self, remember that we must assume our own responsibility, so we are free to exercise the freedom of actions as well as freedom of thinking. Both the clergy and political classes of our people should remember this and preach it. Where are our degreed scholars' and scientists' works in the way of trying to help themselves and their people to self independence? We are a nation in a nation, with a population, according to the census, between 20 to 30 million ex-slaves roaming the country over seeking the master's pity. If we do something for self, we accept our own pity. God will help those who help themselves. Let us unite and agree on simple truth—and get some of this earth wherein we can do for self as other free nations have done.

2. Nonviolence Stands in the Middle of "Do-Nothingism" and Black Nationalist Hatred and Despair.

I have tried to stand between these two forces saying that we need not follow the "do-nothingism" of the complacent or the hatred and despair of the black nationalist. There is the more excellent way of love[77] and nonviolent protest. [78] I'm grateful to God that, through the Negro church, the dimension of nonviolence entered our struggle. [79]

[77] This is a quotation of 1 Corinthians 12:31b, "And now I will show you the most excellent way." This introduces 1 Corinthians 13, Paul's great chapter on love. Verses 1-8 declare, "If I speak in the tongues of men and of angels, but have not love, I am only a resounding gong or a clanging cymbal. If I have the gift of prophecy and can fathom all mysteries and all knowledge and if I have a faith that can move mountains, but have not love, I am nothing. If I give all I possess to the poor and surrender my body to the flames, abut have not love,

I gain nothing. Love is patient, love is kind. It does not envy, it does not boast, it is not proud. It is not rude, it is not self-seeking, it is not easily angered, it keeps no record of wrongs. Love does not delight in evil but rejoices with the truth. It always protects, always trusts, always hopes, always perseveres. Love never fails...."

[78] See notes 26, 34, and 45 above.

[79] Dr. King's "My Pilgrimage to Nonviolence" explains the many viewpoints he considered before embracing nonviolence as his method of addressing injustice. This was deeply compatible with the Negro Church. But along the way, he also considered Marxist teaching, but rejected it as inconsistent with his Christian faith. Dr. King's critique of communism is found in his *Papers*, IV, pp. 475-476. He writes,

> During the Christmas holidays of 1949 I decided to spend my spare time reading Karl Marx to try to understand the appeal of communism for many people. For the first time I carefully scrutinized *Das Kapital* and *The Communist Manifesto*. I also read some interpretive works on the thinking of Marx and Lenin. In reading such Communist writings I drew certain conclusions that have remained with me to this day.
>
> First I rejected their materialistic interpretation of history. Communism, avowedly secularistic and materialistic, has no place for God. This I could never accept, for as a Christian I believe that there is a creative personal power in this universe who is the ground and essence of all reality—a power that cannot be explained in materialistic terms. History is ultimately guided by spirit, not matter.
>
> Second, I strongly disagreed with communism's ethical relativism. Since for the Coummunist there is no divine government, no absolute moral order, there are not fixed, immutable principles; consequently almost anything—force, violence, murder, lying—is a justifiable means to the "millennial" end. This type of relativism was abhorrent to me. Constructive ends can never give absolute moral justification to destructive means, because in the

final analysis the end is preexistent in the mean.

Third, I opposed communism's political totalitarianism. In communism the individual ends up in subjection to the state. True, the Marxist would argue that the state is an "interim" reality which is to be eliminated when the classless society emerges; but the state is the end while it lasts, and man only a means to that end. And if any man's so-called rights or liberties stand in the way of that end, they are simply swept aside. His liberties of expression, his freedom to vote, his freedom to listen to what news he likes or to choose his books are all restricted. Man becomes hardly more, in communism, than a depersonalized cog in the running wheel of the state.

This deprecation of individual freedom was objectionable to me. I am convinced now, as I was then, that man is an end because he is a child of God. Man is not made for the state; the state is made for man. To deprive man of freedom is to relegate him to the status of a thing, rather than elevate him to the status of a person. Man must never be treated as a means to the end of the state, but always as an end within himself.

Yet in spite of the fact that my response to communism was and is negative, and I considered it basically evil, there were points at which I found it challenging. The late Archbishop of Canterbury, William Temple, referred to communism as a Christian heresy. By this he meant that communism had laid hold of certain truths which are essential parts of the Christian view of things, but that it had bound up with them concepts and practices which no Christian could ever accept or profess. Communism challenged the late Archbishop and it should challenge every Christian—as it challenged me—to a growing concern about social justice... The Christian ought always to be challenged by any protest against unfair treatment of the poor, for Christianity is itself such a protest, nowhere expressed more eloquently than in Jesus's words: 'The Spirit of the Lord is upon me, because he hath anointed me to preach the gospel to the poor: He hath sent me to heal the brokenhearted, to preach deliverance to the captives, and recovering of the sight to the blind, to set at liberty them that are bruised, to preach the acceptable year of the Lord."

I also sought systematic answers to Marx's critique of modern bourgeois culture. He presented capitalism as essentially a struggle between the owners of the productive resources and the workers, whom Marx regarded as the real producers. Marx interpreted economic forces as the dialectical process by which society moved from feudalism through capitalism to socialism, with the primary mechanism of this historical movement being the struggle between economic classes whose interest were irreconcilable. Obviously this theory left out of account the numerous and significant complexities—political, economic, moral, religious, and psychological—which played a vital role in shaping the constellation of institutions and ideas known today as Western civilization. Moreover, it was dated in the sense that the capitalism Marx wrote about bore only a partial resemblance to the capitalism we know in this country today. (Dr. King's assessment "borrows both ideas and phrasing from an essay by Robert McCracken, minister at New York's Riverside Church." See Robert J. McCracken, "What Should be the Christian Attitude Toward Comunism?" in Questions People Ask (New York: Harper & Brothers, 1951), pp. 163-172.

3. Nonviolent Action Has Prevented Inevitable Bloodshed.

If this philosophy had not emerged I am convinced that by now many streets of the South would be flowing with floods of blood. And I am further convinced that if our white brothers dismiss us as "rabble rousers" and "outside agitators" -- those of us who are working through the channels of nonviolent direct action -- and refuse to support our nonviolent efforts, millions of Negroes, out of frustration and despair, will seek solace and security in black-nationalist ideologies, a development that will lead inevitably to a frightening racial nightmare.

IV. Alleged Extremism and Actual Extremism.
A. The Oppressed Cannot Stay Silent; Desires for Liberty Will Be Expressed Violently Or Nonviolently.

Oppressed people cannot remain oppressed forever. The urge for freedom will eventually come. This is what has happened to the American Negro. Something within has reminded him of his birthright of freedom; something without has reminded him that he can gain it. Consciously and unconsciously, he has been swept in by what the Germans call the Zeitgeist[80], and with his black brothers of Africa, and his brown and yellow brothers of Asia, South America, and the Caribbean, he is moving with a sense of cosmic urgency toward the promised land of racial justice[81]. Recognizing this vital urge that has engulfed the Negro community, one should readily understand public demonstrations. The Negro has many pent-up resentments and latent frustrations. He has to get them out. So let him march sometime; let him have his prayer pilgrimages to the city hall; understand why he must have sit-ins and freedom rides[82]. If his repressed emotions do not come out in these nonviolent ways, they will come out in ominous expressions of violence. This is not a threat; it is a fact of history. So I have not said to my people, "Get rid of your discontent." But I have tried to say that this normal and healthy discontent can be channeled through the creative outlet of nonviolent direct action. Now this approach is being dismissed as extremist. I must admit that I was initially disappointed in being so categorized.

---

[80] *Zeitgeist* is a word borrowed from German, constructed from the words for "time" (*zeit*) and the word for "spirit" (*geist*). So when it is literally translated it means, "Time-Spirit", or "the spirit of the times." Perhaps better here would be the phrase, "spirit of the age" which focuses its meaning on the worldview, the ethics, the philosophy or cultural values that dominate or characterize a given age or time in the history of human thought.

[81] The image of the "promised land" is a motif that moves through the story of the Old Testament and is especially seen in the Pentateuch, the first five books of the Old Testament. It is implicit in Abram's call in Genesis 12:1, "The Lord had said to Abram, 'Leave your

country, your people and your father's household and go to the land I will show you.'" It is evident in Moses' call to deliver the Israelites in Exodus 3:7-8, "The Lord said, 'I have indeed seen the misery of my people in Egypt. I have heard them crying out because of their slave drivers, and I am concerned about their suffering. So I have come down to rescue them from the hand of the Egyptians and to bring them up out of that land into a good and spacious land, a land flowing with milk and honey....'" Genesis 50:24 records the words of Joseph about the Promised Land, "Then Joseph said to his brother, 'I am about to die. But God will surely come to your aid and take you up out of this land to the land he promised on oath to Abraham, Isaac and Jacob. And Joseph made the sons of Israel swear an oath and said, 'God will surely come to your aid, and then you must carry my bones up from this place.'" Other significant examples include Deuteronomy 11:22-25 and Deuteronomy 19:8. See also, Genesis 24:7; 28:15; 50:24; Exodus 3:17; 12:25; 13:11; 32:13; 33:1; Numbers 1:12; 14:16, 23; 32:11; Deuteronomy 6:3, 18, 23; 8:1; 9:28; 11:22-25; 19:8; 26:15; 27:3; 31:20-23; 34:4.

[82] Student activists began the Freedom Rides to confront segregation on interstate buses and at bus terminals in the spring of 1961. They began their bus rides at Washington, D.C. and headed to Montgomery, Alabama. The students encountered violent resistance as they entered the historically segregated deep southern states of South Carolina and Alabama. This captured national media coverage and helped lead to the action of the Kennedy administration. The Freedom Rides ultimately helped to achieve the desegregation of all buses and terminals under the oversight of the Interstate Commerce Commission.

IV.

B. What Type of Extremism Is Best?: The Christian Model Is Extremism for Love and Justice.

But as I continued to think about the matter I gradually gained a bit of satisfaction from being considered an extremist. Was not Jesus an extremist in love? "Love your enemies, bless them that curse you, pray for them that despitefully use you."[83] Was not Amos an extremist for justice -- "Let justice roll down like waters and righteousness like a mighty stream."[84] Was not Paul an extremist for the gospel of Jesus Christ -- "I bear in my body the marks of the Lord Jesus."[85] Was not Martin Luther an extremist -- "Here I stand; I can do none other so help me God."[86] Was not John Bunyan an extremist -- "I will stay in jail to the end of my days before I make a butchery of my conscience." [87] Was not Abraham Lincoln an extremist -- "This nation cannot survive half slave and half free." [88] Was not Thomas Jefferson an extremist -- "We hold these truths to be self-evident, that all men are created equal." [89] So the question is not whether we will be extremist but what kind of extremist will we be. Will we be extremists for hate or will we be extremists for love? Will we be extremists for the preservation of injustice -- or will we be extremists for the cause of justice? In that dramatic scene on Calvary's hill three men were crucified. [90] We must never forget that all three were crucified for the same crime -- the crime of extremism. Two were extremists for immorality, and thus fell below their environment. [91] The other, Jesus Christ, was an extremist for love, truth, and goodness[92], and thereby rose above His environment[93]. So, after all, maybe the South, the nation, and the world are in dire need of creative extremists[94].

[83] Jesus was an extremist for love, so much so he calls forth love for one's enemies. Dr. King quotes Jesus' words from Matthew 5:44 as found in the KJV. If there were to be a theme verse from Jesus' teaching for a nonviolent engagement with one's enemy, this would surely have to be one of the most appropriate selections.

[84] This is a quotation of the Old Testament minor prophet Amos, taken from Amos 5:24. Amos was an extremist for justice in ancient Israel. Dr. King quotes from the New American Standard Bible in his final version: "Let justice roll down like waters and righteousness like an ever-flowing stream." The public domain version says, "Let justice roll down like waters and righteousness like a mighty stream." This is similar to the American Standard Version that says, "But let justice roll down as waters, and righteousness as a mighty stream."

[85] This is a quotation of Paul from Galatians 6:17 taken from the KJV revealing indeed that Paul was an extremist for the gospel of Christ. The full verse reads, "From henceforth let no man trouble me: for I bear in my body the marks of the Lord Jesus." These words conclude Paul's great defense of the Gospel of justification by faith for both Jew and Gentile in the epistle to the Galatians. He here calls attention to the fact that his authority should not be resisted as it had been by the legalists or Judaizers, those who had called for Christians to return to following Jewish practices prescribed by the Old Testament Law (2:1-5; 11-21). This insistence by Paul that his authority should be respected was not only because of the arguments that he had presented earlier such as his learning these gospel truths directly from the risen Christ (1:11-17) and having received the blessing of the apostle Peter and others to teach and

preach them (1:18-24; 2:1-10). Paul here argues that his authority should be accepted because of his sufferings almost unto death for this gospel of grace, a suffering that was manifested by the visible scars in his body. These scars came from his many sufferings such as his stoning in Lystra (Acts 14:8-23) as well as from the many other tribulations he endured as summarized in 2 Corinthians 11:23-28. These verses in the KJV say, "Are they Hebrews? So am I. Are they Israelites? So am I. Are they the seed of Abraham? So am I. Are they ministers of Christ? (I speak as a fool,) I am more; in labors more abundant, in stripes above measure, in prisons more frequent, in deaths oft. Of the Jews five times received I forty stripes save one. Thrice was I beaten with rods, once was I stoned, thrice I suffered shipwreck, a night and a day I have been in the deep; in journeyings often, in perils of waters, in perils of robbers, in perils by mine own countrymen, in perils by the heathen, in perils in the city, in perils in the wilderness, in perils in the sea, in perils among false brethren; in weariness and painfulness, in watchings often, in hunger and thirst, in fastings often , in cold and nakedness. Beside those things that are without, that which cometh upon me daily, the care of all the churches."

[86] The story of Luther shows that he was an extremist for the Word of God. Luther at the Imperial Diet of Worms on April 18, 1528 declared: "Unless I am convicted by Scripture and plain reason---I do not accept the authority of popes and councils, for they have contradicted each other---my conscience is captive to the Word of God. I cannot and I will not recant anything, for to go against conscience is neither right nor safe. Here I stand, I cannot do otherwise. God help me, Amen." Some claim that the famous saying "Here I stand. I cannot do otherwise." does not come from Luther. Nevertheless, the memorial statue of Martin Luther in the city of Worms bears the famous words: Here I stand, I cannot do otherwise, so help me God. Amen."

The Diet of Worms was a specially called national congress where Luther defended his doctrines that were at the heart of the Reformation, even though the church and Emperor wanted Luther to recant his teachings while he was there. Due to the church's excommunication before Luther was invited to Worms, he had already in essence been declared a heretic. On his journey to Worms, Luther was welcomed in all of the towns he went through, preaching along the way. He arrived in Worms on April 16 and was also cheered and welcomed by the people. Luther appeared before the Emperor twice. At each time he was told to recant. But Luther refused since he did not see any evidence that his teachings were unbiblical.

When Luther was dismissed, he was not arrested because he had a letter of safe conduct which guaranteed three weeks of safe travel. He left for home on April 25. But when Luther and his protecting princes departed, the emperor imposed an Imperial Act wherein Luther was declared an outlaw. This meant that he could be slain by anyone without fear of reprisal. So Elector Friedrich the Wise had Luther kidnapped on May 4th to assure Luther's safety. Luther was taken to the Wartburg Castle where he remained for ten months. After only three months there he had translated the New Testament into German. Later he translated the complete Old Testament into German.

[87] John Bunyan models extremism for his conscience and for his faith. Dr. King here paraphrases a line from John Bunyan (1628-1688), the famous author of *Pilgrim's Progress*. Dr. Joel Beeke and Randall J. Pederson give us the actual quote of Bunyan in this citation from their work, *Meet the Puritans*:

> In 1666, the middle of his prison-time, he wrote *Grace Abounding to the Chief of Sinners*, in which he declared, "The Almighty God being my help and shield, I am determined yet to suffer, if frail life might continue so long, even till the moss shall grow upon my eyebrows, rather than violate my faith and principles."

Clearly Bunyan was an extremist for living out his faith in the Word of God. John Owen said of John Bunyan, a powerful preacher and the best-known of all the Puritan writers, that he would gladly exchange all his learning for Bunyan's power of touching men's hearts. Beeke and Pederson summarize the highpoints of the history of Bunyan's conversion and Christian life:

> In 1651, the women introduced Bunyan to John Gifford, their pastor in Bedford. God used Gifford to lead Bunyan to repentance and faith. Bunyan was particularly influenced by a sermon Gifford preached on Song of Solomon 4:1, "Behold thou art fair, my love, behold thou art fair," as well as by reading Luther's commentary of Galatians, in which he found his own experience "largely

and profoundly handled, as if [Luther's] book had been written out of my own heart" (cited by Greaves, John Bunyan, p. 18). While walking through a field one day, Christ's righteousness was revealed to Bunyan's soul and gained the victory. Bunyan writes of that unforgettable experience:

One day, as I was passing in the field, this sentence fell upon my soul: Thy righteousness is in heaven; and methought withal I saw with the eyes of my soul, Jesus Christ, at God's right hand; there, I say, as my righteousness; so that wherever I was, or whatever I was a-doing, God could not say of me, He wants my righteousness, for that was just before Him. I also saw, moreover, that it was not my good frame of heart that made my righteousness better, nor yet my bad frame that made my righteousness worse; for my righteousness was Jesus Christ Himself, the same yesterday, today, and forever. Now did my chains fall off my legs indeed. I was loosed from my afflictions and irons; my temptations also fled away. Now I went home rejoicing for the grace and love of God. I lived for some time very sweetly at peace with God through Christ. Oh! methought, Christ! Christ! There was nothing but Christ that was before my eyes. I saw now not only looking upon this and the other benefits of Christ apart, as of His blood, burial, and resurrection, but considered Him as a whole Christ! It was glorious to me to see His exaltation, and the worth and prevalency of all His benefits, and that because now I could look from myself to Him, and would reckon that all those graces of God that now were green in me, were yet but like those cracked groats and fourpence-halfpennies that rich men carry in their purses, when their gold is in their trunk at home! Oh, I saw that my gold was in my trunk at home! In Christ my Lord and Saviour! Now Christ was all (Grace Abounding, paragraphs 229-32, pp. 129-31)....

In 1660, while preaching in a farmhouse at Lower Samsell, Bunyan was arrested on the charge of preaching without official rights from the king. When told that he would be freed if he no longer preached, he replied, "If I am freed today, I will preach tomorrow." He was thrown into prison, where he wrote prolifically and made shoelaces to provide some income for twelve and a half years (1660-1672).

Prior to his arrest, Bunyan had remarried, this time to a godly young woman named Elizabeth. She pleaded repeatedly for his release, but judges such as Sir Matthew Hale and Thomas Twisden rejected her plea. So Bunyan remained in prison with no formal charge and no legal sentence, in defiance of the habeas corpus provisions of the Magna Carta, because he refused to give up preaching the gospel and denounced the Church of England as false (see Bunyan's A Relation of My Imprisonment, published posthumously in 1765). In 1661 and from 1668-1672, certain jailers permitted Bunyan to leave prison at times to preach. George Offer notes, "It is said that many of the Baptist congregations in Bedfordshire owe their origins to his midnight preaching" (Works of Bunyan, 1:lix). His prison years were times of difficult trials, however. Bunyan experienced what his Pilgrim's Progress characters Christian and Faithful would later suffer at the hands of Giant Despair, who thrust pilgrim "into a very dark dungeon, nasty and stinking." Bunyan especially felt the pain of separation from his wife and children, particularly "blind Mary," describing it as a "pulling of the flesh from my bones."

Prison years, however, were productive years for Bunyan. In the mid-1660s, Bunyan wrote extensively, with only the Bible and Foxe's Book of Martyrs at his side. In 1663, he wrote Christian Behaviour, intended as a handbook for Christian living and a response against charges of antinomianism, as well as a last testament, since Bunyan expected to die in prison. He also finished I Will Pray with the Spirit, which expounded 1 Corinthians 14:15, and focused on the Spirit's inner work in all true prayer. In 1664, he published Profitable Meditations; in 1665, One Thing Needful, The Holy City (his understanding of church history and the end times), and The Resurrection of the Dead. This latter work is a sequel to The Holy City, in which Bunyan expounds the resurrection from Acts 24:14-15 in a traditional way, and then uses his prison torments to illustrate the horrors that await the damned following the final judgment. In 1666, the middle of his prison-time, he wrote Grace Abounding to the Chief of Sinners, in which he declared, "The Almighty God being my help and shield, I am determined yet to suffer, if frail life might continue so long, even till the moss shall grow upon my eyebrows, rather than violate my faith and principles."

[88] Abraham Lincoln's words reflect extremism for the civil liberty of the slave. They were received as extreme in his day and cost him his bid to be elected to the US Senate representing Illinois. For examples of the assertion of President Abraham Lincoln quoted by Dr. King, consider the following two items.

October 13, 1858: Sixth Debate with Stephen A. Douglas, Quincy, Illinois *In the Lincoln-Douglas debates, Douglas maintained that the Founding Fathers established this nation half-slave and half-free in the belief that it would always be so. Lincoln argued that the Founding Fathers considered slavery wrong, and firmly expected it to die a natural death.*

I wish to return Judge Douglas my profound thanks for his public annunciation here to-day, to be put on record, that his system of policy in regard to the institution of slavery contemplates that it shall last forever. We are getting a little nearer the true issue of this controversy, and I am profoundly grateful for this one sentence. Judge Douglas asks you "why cannot the institution of slavery, or rather, why cannot the nation, part slave and part free, continue as our fathers made it forever?" In the first place, I insist that our

fathers did not make this nation half slave and half free, or part slave and part free. I insist that they found the institution of slavery existing here. They did not make it so, but they left it so because they knew of no way to get rid of it at that time. When Judge Douglas undertakes to say that as a matter of choice the fathers of the government made this nation part slave and part free, he assumes what is historically a falsehood. More than that; when the fathers of the government cut off the source of slavery by the abolition of the slave trade, and adopted a system of restricting it from the new Territories where it had not existed, I maintain that they placed it where they understood, and all sensible men understood, it was in the course of ultimate extinction; and when Judge Douglas asks me why it cannot continue as our fathers made it, I ask him why he and his friends could not let it remain as our fathers made it?
Collected Works of Abraham Lincoln (Abraham Lincoln Association), Vol. III, p. 276.

House Divided speech, Springfield, Illinois, June 16 1858.
Lincoln presented the speech to more than 1,000 Republican delegates in the Illinois statehouse at the Republican State Convention only hours after they chose his as their candidate for the U.S. Senate, running against Democrat Stephen A. Douglas. The title of the speech reflects a line in its introduction, "A house divided against itself cannot stand," a quotation from Jesus found in the first three gospels of Matthew, Mark, Luke. His bold message was perceived as too radical by many including some of his closest advisors. He lost the Senate election, but was subsequently elected as President and lived to see both the division of the United States over slavery and the reuniting of the States through the Northern States' victory in the Civil War. The speech begins as follows:

Mr. President and Gentlemen of the Convention.
If we could first know *where* we are, and *whither* we are tending, we could then better judge *what* to do, and *how* to do it. We are now far into the *fifth* year, since a policy was initiated, with the *avowed* object, and *confident* promise, of putting an end to slavery agitation. Under the operation of that policy, that agitation has not only, *not ceased*, but has *constantly augmented*. In *my* opinion, it *will* not cease, until a *crisis* shall have been reached, and passed. "A house divided against itself cannot stand." I believe this government cannot endure, permanently half *slave* and half *free*. I do not expect the Union to be *dissolved* -- I do not expect the house to *fall* -- but

I *do* expect it will cease to be divided. It will become *all* one thing or *all* the other.

[89] Thomas Jefferson's immortal words reflect an extremism for liberty. The Declaration of Independence begins:

> In CONGRESS, July 4, 1776
> The unanimous Declaration of the thirteen United States of America,
>
> When in the Course of human events, it becomes necessary for one people to dissolve the political bands which have connected them with another, and to assume among the powers of the earth, the separate and equal station to which the Laws of Nature and of Nature's God entitle them, a decent respect to the opinions of mankind requires that they should declare the causes which impel them to the separation.
>
> We hold these truths to be self-evident, that all men are created equal, that they are endowed by their Creator with certain unalienable Rights, that among these are Life, Liberty, and the pursuit of Happiness. That to secure these rights, Governments are instituted among Men, deriving their just powers from the consent of the governed. That whenever any Form of Government becomes destructive of these ends, it is the Right of the People to alter or to abolish it, and to institute new Government, laying its foundation on such principles and organizing its powers in such form, as to them shall seem most likely to effect their Safety and Happiness.
>
> Prudence, indeed, will dictate that Governments long established should not be changed for light and transient causes; and accordingly all experience hath shewn, that mankind are more disposed to suffer, while evils are sufferable, than to right themselves by abolishing the forms to which they are accustomed.
>
> But when a long train of abuses and usurpations, pursuing invariably the same object evinces a design to reduce them under absolute

Despotism, it is their right, it is their duty, to throw off such Government, and to provide new Guards for their future security.

Such has been the patient sufferance of these Colonies; and such is now the necessity which constrains them to alter their former Systems.

[90] The Gospels record the story of the crucifixion of three men at the same time and place with Jesus in the middle. Matthew 27:38 says, "Two robbers were crucified with him, one on his right and one on his left." (See Mark 15:27). Luke 23:32, 39-42 says, "Two other men, both criminals, were also led out with him to be executed. One of the criminals who hung there hurled insults at him: 'Aren't you the Christ? Save yourself and us!' But the other criminal rebuked him. 'Don't you fear God,' he said, 'since you are under the same sentence? We are punished justly, for we are getting what our deeds deserve. But this man has done nothing wrong.' The he said, 'Jesus, remember me when you come into your kingdom.' Jesus answered him, 'I tell you the truth, today you will be with me in paradise.'" John 19:18 says, "Here they crucified him, and with him two others—one on each side and Jesus in the middle." These accounts of the crucifixion show us that one of the criminals who had "fallen below his environment" also was to be lifted up with Christ "above his environment" because of faith in in Christ.

[91] "Fell" is a suggestive word by which perhaps Dr. King intends to remind the reader of humanity's "fall" into sin. This is the theological word to describe the entrance of sin into the world as found in Genesis 3 with the disobedience of Adam and Eve. The two crucified with Christ who fell below their environment as "extremists for immorality" are identified in the texts just cited in the previous note as "robbers" and "criminals". Examples of moral falling and its consequences in Scripture are: Luke 10:18, "He replied, 'I saw Satan fall like lightning from heaven.'" Romans 11:22, "Consider therefore the kindness and sternness of God: sternness to those who fell, but kindness to you, provided that you continue in his kindness. Otherwise, you also will be cut off." I Corinthians 10:12-13 "So, if you think you are standing firm, be careful that you don't fall! No temptation has seized you except what is common to man. And God is faithful; he will not let you be tempted beyond what you can bear. But when you are tempted, he will also provide a way out so that you can stand up under it." Revelation 18:2, "With a mighty voice he shouted: 'Fallen! Fallen is Babylon the Great! She

has become a home for demons and a haunt for every evil spirit, a haunt for every unclean and detestable bird." Jude 24, "To him who is able to keep you from falling and to present you before his glorious presence without fault and great joy—to the only God our Savior be glory, majesty, power and authority through Jesus Christ our Lord, before all ages, now and forevermore! Amen."

[92] According to Dr. King, Jesus was an extremist for "love, truth and goodness". Jesus' extreme love is seen in His teaching and in His life. His extremism for love is seen in His call for His followers to love their enemies as Dr. King cited Matthew 5:44. (See note 82 above.) His extremism for love is seen in His *life* in His giving His life for His sheep (John 10:7-18). John 13:1, "Having loved his own who were in the world, he now showed them the full extent of his love."

Jesus' extreme truth is seen in His teaching and in His life. His extremism for truth is seen in His *life* in the words that were spoken to Him by his opponents. Matthew 22:16, "They sent their disciples to him along with the Herodians. 'Teacher,' they said, 'we know you are a man of integrity and that you teach the way of God in accordance with the truth. You aren't swayed by men, because you pay no attention to who they are." His extremism for truth is seen in His *teaching* in His declaration in John 14:6, "Jesus answered, 'I am the way and the truth and the life. No one comes to the Father except through me."

Jesus' extreme goodness is seen in His teaching and in His life. Jesus' extreme goodness is seen in His *teaching* and in His *life* in His classic words about His sacrificial death for His people in John 10:11-15, "I am the good shepherd. The good shepherd lays down his life for the sheep. The hired hand is not the shepherd who owns the sheep. So when he sees the wolf coming, he abandons the sheep and runs away. Then the wolf attacks the flock and scatters it. The man runs away because he is a hired hand and he cares nothing for the sheep. I am the good shepherd; I know my sheep and my sheep know me…and I lay down my life for the sheep."

[93] "Rose" here is a play on words hinting at the resurrection of Jesus who "rose" from the dead. Jesus not just "rose" above his environment; He also rose from the grave according to the Gospels: Matthew 28:6, "He is not here; he has risen, just as he said." Mark 16:6, "Don't be alarmed,' he said. 'You are looking for Jesus the Nazarene, who was crucified. He has risen! He is not here." Luke 24:6, "He is not here; he has risen! Remember how he told you, while he was still with you in Galilee: The Son of Man must be delivered into the hands of sinful men, be crucified and on the third day be raised again.'"

Paul writes, "We believe that Jesus died and rose again...." (1 Thessalonians 4:14.)

[94] The concept of a "creative extremist" is the conclusion of this series of examples used by Dr. King—Amos (justice), Paul (gospel), Luther (Scripture), Bunyan (conscience), Lincoln (manumission of slaves), Jefferson (political liberty). But we should also notice that the first and the last of Dr. King's appeals are to Jesus Christ (love for one's enemy). This rhetorical device not only reflects Dr. King's commitment to nonviolence but also reflects a metaphorical name given to Jesus Christ in the Scriptures, "the first and the Last, the beginning and the end" (Revelation 1:17; 21:6; 22:12-13). Jesus Christ in His call for the love of one's enemies, and then His being crucified on the cross by His enemies and thereby manifesting the love of God (John 3:16), reveal why Jesus is the consummate creative extremist in Dr. King's mind. Jesus is the creative extremist because He gave a new, creative and extreme meaning to love, truth and goodness by His teaching and His cross. Thus Dr. King presents the need for others to walk in Jesus' steps and to imitate Him by seeking new ways to rise above the world as we know it, by pursuing extreme expressions of love, truth and goodness. Scriptural teaching to this effect includes: I Peter 2:21, "To this you were called, because Christ suffered for you, leaving you an example, that you should follow in his steps." 1 John 2:5-6, "But if anyone obeys his word, God's love is truly made complete in him. This is how we know we are in him: Whoever claims to live in him must walk as Jesus did."

V. Disappointment with White Moderates and the Church.
A. A Minister's Expression of Love for the Church and Disappointment at the White Church's Silence.
1. Perhaps Too Optimistic That White Moderates Would See the Need, Thankful That Some Have Helped.

I had hoped that the white moderate would see this. Maybe I was too optimistic. Maybe I expected too much. I guess I should have realized that few members of a race that has oppressed another race can understand or appreciate the deep groans and passionate yearnings of those that have been oppressed, and still fewer have the vision to see that injustice must be rooted out by strong, persistent, and determined action. I am thankful, however, that some of our white brothers have grasped the meaning of this social revolution and committed themselves to it. They are still all too small in quantity, but they are big in quality. Some like Ralph McGill[95],

Lillian Smith[96], Harry Golden[97], and James Dabbs[98] [99] [100] have written about our struggle in eloquent, prophetic, and understanding terms. Others have marched with us down nameless streets of the South. They have languished in filthy, roach-infested jails, suffering the abuse and brutality of angry policemen who see them as "dirty nigger lovers." They, unlike so many of their moderate brothers and sisters, have recognized the urgency of the moment and sensed the need for powerful "action" antidotes to combat the disease of segregation.

[95] Ralph McGill, Lillian Smith, Harry Golden, James McBride Dabbs, Ann Braden and Sarah Patton Boyle were writers who sought to address the evils of segregation. Ralph McGill (1898-1969) was the editor and publisher of the Atlanta Constitution, and a major leader for racial respect in the South. He was the first major southern columnist to openly discuss ending segregation. McGill published *A Church, a School* (1959), compiled from his Pulitzer Prize winning editorials on the Atlanta Temple bombing and on the hate crimes of the Ku Klux Klan.

[96] Lillian Smith (1897-1966) was one of the first prominent white southerners to denounce racial segregation openly and to work actively against it. From as early as the 1930s, she argued that enforced racial laws were evil. She wrote *Strange Fruit* (1944) a novel with the theme of illicit interracial love. She also wrote *Killers of the Dream* (1949) warning that segregation corrupted the soul and southern society. By the 1955 Montgomery, Alabama, bus boycott Smith had conversed with many southern blacks concerning the conditions in which they lived. She corresponded with civil rights leader Martin Luther King Jr. openly supporting his efforts. Her last published work was *Our Faces, Our Words* (1964), which celebrated the nonviolence efforts of the civil rights movement.

[97] The Jewish-American Harry Golden (1902-1981) was writer and publisher of the *Carolina Israelite* and author of *Only in America*. After a checkered background in the investment world, Golden turned to writing. The *Carolina Israelite* began in 1942 addressing controversial issues such as racial integration. Golden collected his *Carolina Israelite* articles into his book, *Only in America* (1958) which became a bestseller. He was known for his humor as he addressed the challenging societal issues facing the south. By the late '60s Golden rejected the extremism of the civil rights movement, resigning from the Student Nonviolent Coordinating Committee (SNCC) because of its opposition to Israel.

[98] James McBride Dabbs was a South Carolinian, president of the

Southern Regional Council, and author of *The Southern Heritage*. In an interview with Mike Wallace in 1958, he openly addressed segregation and school integration. A portion of that interview follows:

> WALLACE: This is James McBride Dabbs, President of the Southern Regional Council, which is a group of Southerners, both Negro and white, who are leading the fight against racial conflict in the South. A native of South Carolina, Mr. Dabbs says of the South: "The Negro is always with us as we are with him. There he is before our eyes, the symbol of our sin, the living reminder to our hearts that our words are wrong." ...
>
> WALLACE: ... Mr. Dabbs, you write in your book something very intriguing. You say, "We don't admit this, of course, but the fact remains that the Negro has been the dominant force in Southern life since 1865." And you say, "Though the problem has been out of sight, its shadow has remained, to darken our minds and dampen our spirits." What does that mean?
>
> DABBS: That means, as I understand it, that we Southerners are democratic, along with the rest of the Americans, and when, following the Civil War and Reconstruction, we clamped segregation and disfranchisement down upon the Negro against his will -- we never asked him anything about it -- er... we had, and have, the sense of doing an undemocratic thing. We may have called it necessity or whatnot, but we know deep down this isn't the way Americans act, and therefore we have really a bad conscience about the matter. We have pressed this thing down. We don't take it into the open and face it. And therefore, it forever shapes and colors all of our opinions and actions.
>
> WALLACE: Mr. Dabbs, ... who are the men in the South who are the leaders whom you respect and who can lead the South to a better understanding of our racial problem?
>
> DABBS: Well, the men I think of are the men I am more or less associated with in the Southern

Regional Council. I think of both Negroes and whites....

WALLACE: Martin Luther King?

DABBS: Martin Luther King, of course, one of the outstanding figures of the South, the Montgomery episode is absolutely unprecedented.

[99] In the final version Dr. King adds the name of Ann Braden. Anne McCarty Braden (1924 – 2006) was raised in Alabama and became an advocate of racial equality. In 1948 she married newspaperman Carl Braden, and joined him in support of the civil rights movement. Ostracized for their beliefs, they were hired by the Southern Conference Educational Fund, a New Orleans-based civil rights organization whose mission was to seek white southern support for the civil rights movement. They published *The Southern Patriot* to spread the news about major civil rights campaigns. In 1958 Anne wrote *The Wall Between* which was appreciated by Martin Luther King Jr. and was a runner-up for the National Book Award.

[100] In the final version Dr. King adds the name of Sarah-Patton Boyle (1906–1994). She was a prominent Virginian white civil rights activists during the 1950s and 1960s. She wrote The Desegregated Heart: A Virginian's Stand in Time of Transition (1962). Her work with the University of Virginia's first black law student changed her views of gradual desegregation to a position of immediate desegregation in public schools and in higher education. Her 1955 article "Southerners Will Like Integration," created a racial protest included a cross burned in her Charlottesville yard. Boyle continued her efforts for desegregation by laboring with the National Association for the Advancement of Colored People (NAACP), which earned the esteem of Martin Luther King Jr. With the impact of personal depression and the powerful struggles of the civil rights movement, she eventually became disillusioned and retired from activism in 1967.

2. Disappoint with the White Church and Its Leadership, with some Notable Exceptions.

Let me rush on to mention my other disappointment. I have been so greatly disappointed with the white Church and its leadership. Of course there are some notable exceptions. I am not unmindful of the fact that each of you has taken some significant stands on this issue. I commend you, Rev. Stallings, for your Christian stand on this past Sunday, in welcoming

Negroes to your worship service on a non-segregated basis[101]. I commend the Catholic leaders of this state for integrating Spring Hill College several years ago. [102]

> [101] For a discussion of Rev. Stallings, see note 9 above.
>
> [102] In 1954 prior to the Supreme Court's Brown decision, Spring Hill College, the oldest Jesuit college in the South, became the first college in Alabama to integrate its student body.

3. This Disappointment With the Church Is from A Minister of the Gospel Who Will Always Be True to It.

But despite these notable exceptions I must honestly reiterate that I have been disappointed with the Church. I do not say that as one of those negative critics who can always find something wrong with the Church. I say it as a minister of the gospel, who loves the Church; who was nurtured in its bosom; who has been sustained by its spiritual blessings and who will remain true to it as long as the cord of life shall lengthen. [103]

> [103] Dr. King's allusion "as long as the cord of life shall lengthen" is an allusion to his eventual death as a mere mortal. He is referring to Ecclesiastes 12:5-7, "…because man goeth to his long home, and the mourners go about the streets: or ever the silver cord be loosed, or the golden bowl be broken, or the pitcher be broken at the fountain, or the wheel broken at the cistern. Then shall the dust return to the earth as it was and the spirit shall return unto God who gave it." His cord of life ceased to be lengthened when he was killed by a gunman in April 1968 almost five years after the *Letter From Birmingham Jail* was written.

4. The White Church: Outright Opponents, Others Have Been More Cautious Than Courageous Remaining Silent behind the Anesthetizing Security of Stained-Glass Windows.

I had the strange feeling when I was suddenly catapulted into the leadership of the bus protest in Montgomery[104] several years ago that we would have the support of the white Church. I felt that the white ministers, priests, and rabbis of the South would be some of our strongest allies. Instead, some have been outright opponents, refusing to understand the freedom movement and misrepresenting its leaders; all too many others have been more cautious than courageous and have remained silent behind the anesthetizing security of the stained glass windows.

[104] The Montgomery bus boycott was an eleven-month protest ignited by the arrest of Rosa Parks on December 1, 1955. It concluded with the U.S. Supreme Court ruling that public bus segregation is unconstitutional. Under the leadership of Martin Luther King, Jr., The Montgomery Improvement Association coordinated the boycott. The bus boycott demonstrated the power of nonviolent protest to defeat racial segregation. In efforts to break the boycott, the homes of Dr. King and Ralph Abernathy were bombed. With the Supreme Court's ruling, on December 21, 1956, the boycott ended. Dr. King's tactics of combining a large scale nonviolent protest with a Christian tone became the method for challenging racial segregation. Dr. King wrote *Stride Toward Freedom* in 1958 to tell the story of the Montgomery bus boycott.

5. Disappointment Expressed That the White Church Did Not Understand the Justice of This Cause and Did Not Help Bring These Just Grievances to the Power Structure.

In spite of my shattered dreams[105] of the past, I came to Birmingham with the hope that the white religious leadership of this community would see the justice of our cause and with deep moral concern, serve as the channel through which our just grievances could get to the power structure. I had hoped that each of you would understand. But again I have been disappointed.

[105] He refers here to his "shattered dreams" but his greatest speech is his "I have a dream"! See Endnote 154.

B. An Unfulfilled Longing: To Hear, "Integration Is Morally Right Because the Negro Is Your Brother."
1. "Those Are Social Issues, with Which the Gospel Has No Real Concern." This Completely Other Worldly Religion Makes a Strange, Unbiblical Distinction between Body and Soul, between the Sacred and Secular.

I have heard numerous religious leaders of the South call upon their worshippers to comply with a desegregation decision because it is the law, but I have longed to hear white ministers say follow this decree because integration is morally right and the Negro is your brother. [106] In the midst of blatant injustices inflicted upon the Negro, I have watched white churches stand on the sideline and merely mouth pious irrelevancies and sanctimonious trivialities. In the midst of a mighty struggle to rid our nation of racial and economic injustice, I have heard so many ministers say, "Those are social issues with which the gospel has no real concern," [107] and I have watched so many churches commit themselves to a completely other-worldly religion which made a strange distinction between body and soul, the sacred and the secular. [108]

So here we are moving toward the exit of the twentieth century with a religious community largely adjusted to the status quo, standing as a tail-light behind other community agencies rather than a headlight leading men to higher levels of justice.

[106] For a discussion of the ideas of moral law and natural law versus positive law, see notes 42 and 52 above. The phrase "Because the Negro is my brother" is reflective of the Christmas Carol, "O Holy Night" composed by Unitarian minister Adolphe Adam in 1847 to the French poem "Minuit, Chrétiens" (Midnight, Christians) which includes the phrase "because the slave is my brother". The French text was written by Placid Cappeau (1808–1877), a poet, who had been asked by a parish priest to write a Christmas poem. John Sullivan Dwight editor of *Dwight's Journal of Music*, created a singing edition of the words based on Cappeau's French text in 1855. The lyrics follow with the relevant section from Dr. King's *Letter* highlighted:

> *O holy night! The stars are brightly shining,*
> *It is the night of our dear Saviour's birth.*
> *Long lay the world in sin and error pining,*
> *'Til He appear'd and the soul felt its worth.*
> *A thrill of hope the weary world rejoices,*
> *For yonder breaks a new and glorious morn.*
> *Fall on your knees! O hear the angels' voices!*
> *O night divine, O night when Christ was born;*
> *O night divine, O night, O night Divine.*
>
> *Led by the light of Faith serenely beaming,*
> *With glowing hearts by His cradle we stand.*
> *So led by light of a star sweetly gleaming,*
>
> *Here come the wise men from Orient land.*
> *The King of Kings lay thus in lowly manger;*

In all our trials born to be our friend.
He knows our need, to our weakness is no stranger,
Behold your King! Before Him lowly bend!
Behold your King, Before Him lowly bend!

Truly He taught us to love one another;
His law is love and His gospel is peace.
Chains shall He break for the slave is our brother;
And in His name all oppression shall cease.
Sweet hymns of joy in grateful chorus raise we,
Let all within us praise His holy name.
Christ is the Lord! O praise His Name forever,
His power and glory evermore proclaim.
His power and glory evermore proclaim.

[107] Dr. King's complaint here touches on an important debate within the Presbyterian tradition. There has been a substantial difference of perspective between those who view the Church's primary calling to be spiritual in focus, "the Spirituality of the Church" and those who hold to a measured degree of activism or "prophetic witness" by the Church in the social and political arena. The Southern Presbyterian tradition emphasized the spirituality of the church viewpoint. One of its leading Civil War era theologians, James Henry Thornwell, affirmed the thesis "Whether slavery exists or not is a question which exclusively belongs to the State". In this context he argued, "We have no right, as a church, to enjoin as a duty, or to condemn it as a sin....The social, civil, political problems connected with this great subject transcend our sphere, as God has not entrusted to his Church the organization of society, the construction of Government, nor the allotment of individuals to their various stations." (Address to the Presbyterian Church in the Confederate States of America, 1861.)

The Northern Presbyterian tradition has differed from Thornwell's view of the spirituality of the Church and has been greatly impacted by the theological position of Charles Hodge. Hodge was in the Northern Presbyterian tradition having been born in Pennsylvania and served for many years as Professor of Systematic Theology at Princeton in the 1800's. Early in his career, he was supportive of the position that defended the legitimacy of slavery, but by 1846, he openly declared that slavery was morally wrong:

Slavery is a heinous crime; it degrades human beings into things; it forbids marriages; it destroys domestic relations; it separates parents and children, husbands and wives; it legalizes what God forbids, and forbids what God enjoins; it keeps its victims in ignorance even of the gospel; it denies labor its wages, subject the persons, the virtue, and the happiness of many to the caprice of one; it involves the violation of all social rights and duties, and therefore is the greatest of social crimes. It is as much as any man's character for sense, honesty or religion is worth, to insist that a distinction must here be made; that we must discriminate between slavery and its separable adjuncts; between the relationship itself and the abuse of it; between the possession of power and the unjust exercise of it. Let any man in some portions of our country, in England, in Scotland, or Ireland, attempt to make such distinctions, and see with what an outburst of indignation he will be overwhelmed. It is just so in the present case. (Charles Hodge, *The Princeton Review*, April 1846).

Furthermore, in his *Systematic Theology*, he rejected the theory that blacks were not fully human, and thus not made in the image of God, one of the arguments that was used by some to justify slavery:

"Whenever we meet a man, no matter of what name or nation, we not only find that he has the same nature with ourselves; that he has the same organs, the same senses, the same instincts, the same feelings, the same faculties, the same understanding, will, and conscience, and the same capacity for religious culture, but that he has the same guilty and polluted nature, and needs the same redemption. Christ died for all men, and we are commanded to preach the gospel to every creature under heaven. Accordingly, nowhere on the face of the earth are men to be found who do not need the gospel or who are not capable of becoming partakers of the blessings which it offers. (Charles Hodge, *Systematic Theology*, 1872, Volume II, pp. 90-91).

Moreover, the Northern Presbyterian tradition has affirmed that it is appropriate for the church to address the civil magistrate in moral issues raised by governmental actions. For example, Westminster Theological Seminary Professor John Murray, a member of the Orthodox Presbyterian Church, born in Scotland and trained at Princeton, called for the Church to speak into the moral arena inclusive of the state, while being careful not to become a political entity:

> When laws are proposed or enacted that are contrary to the Word of God, it is the duty of the church in proclamation and in official pronouncement to oppose and condemn them. . . . It is misconception of what is involved in the proclamation of the whole counsel of God to suppose or plead that the church has no concern with the political sphere. The church is concerned with every sphere and is obligated to proclaim and inculcate the revealed will of God as it bears upon every department of life." (John Murray, "The Church, Its Identity, Function, and Resources" in *The Collected Writings of John Murray*, vol. 1 (Banner of Truth, 1976), p. 241.)
>
> "To the church is committed the task of proclaiming the whole counsel of God and, therefore, the counsel of God as it bears upon the responsibility of all persons and institutions. While the church is not to discharge the functions of other institutions such as the state and the family, nevertheless it is charged to define what the functions of these institutions are. . . . To put the matter bluntly, the church is not to engage in politics. Its members must do so, but only in their capacity as citizens of the state, not as members of the church." (John Murray, "The Relation of Church and State," in *The Collected Writings of John Murray*, vol. 1 (Banner of Truth, 1976), p. 255.)

[108] The struggle to unite body and soul and to join the concern for this world with the concerns of the world to come have been a perpetual issue in Christian thought and practice. Early Church asceticism, Medieval monasticism, Reformation era Anabaptist, Amish and Pietist movements and various modern forms of Christian Fundamentalism are examples of Christian rejections of this worldly concerns for a predominant focus on the world to come. Their criticisms have raised authentic concerns about the this-world focus of liberal Protestantism as well as what they view to be the too closely linked varieties of historic Catholicism and Orthodox Communions with the activities of civil governments. The Fundamentalist critique of these Church movements is twofold. The first is that their social/political activism has led to a loss of Gospel proclamation and passionate concern for the eternal destinies of the souls of men. The second is the loss of the personal and corporate godliness called for by Scripture due to the Church's commitment to the rough and tumble politics of partisan agendas.

Various forms of Evangelical and Reformed traditions have sought to affirm legitimacy for the Church to carry out both the Gospel and the social duties that seem to be enjoined by the teachings of Christ. Such texts as Matthew 5:13-16 and John 17:8-19 are considered to be germane for this approach.

Matthew 5:13-16 affirms, "You are the salt of the earth. But if the salt loses its saltiness, how can it be made salty again? It is no longer good for anything, except to be thrown out and trampled by men. You are the light of the world. A city on a hill cannot be hidden. Neither do people light a lamp and put it under a bowl. Instead they put it on its stand, and it gives light to everyone in the house. In the same way, let your light shine before men, that they may see your good deeds and praise your Father in heaven."

John 17:8-14 states, "For I gave them the words you gave me and they accepted them. They knew with certainty that I came from you, and they believed that you sent me. ...I will remain in the world no longer, but they are still in the world, and I am coming to you. Holy Father, protect them by the power of your name—the name you gave me—so that they may be one as we are one. While I was with them, I protected them and kept them safe by that name you gave me....I am coming to you now, but I say these things while I am still in the world, so that they may have the full measure of my joy within them. I have given them your word and the world has hated them, for they are not of the world any more than I am of the world. My prayer is not that you take them out of the world but that you protect them from the evil one. They are not of the world even as I am not of it. Sanctify them by the truth; your word is truth. As you sent me into the world, I have sent them into the world. For them I sanctify myself that they too may be truly sanctified."

Thus Christians are in the world, but not of the world. They are the salt of the earth and the light of the world. These concepts have led to the view that ultimately, there is to be no distinction for the believer between the sacred and the secular. All that the Christian touches is to be influenced by his or her presence as Christ's salt and light. The believer is truly in the world and thus seeks to impact it, yet all the while doing so by not being of this world.

Finally, Paul explains the idea of a this-worldly impact with an other-worldly methodology in 2 Corinthians 10:3-5, "For though we live in the world, we do not wage war as the world does. The weapons we fight with are not the weapons of the world. On the contrary, they have divine power to demolish strongholds. We demolish arguments and every pretension that sets itself up against the knowledge of God, and we take captive every thought to make it obedient to Christ."

A famous saying attributed to Abraham Kuyper (1837-1920) seems to proclaim this perspective well, "There is not a square inch in the whole domain of our human existence over which Christ, who is Sovereign over all, does not cry: 'Mine!'"

2. The South's Lovely Churches: Where Were Their Voices When Negroes Rose to Protest?

I have travelled the length and breadth of Alabama, Mississippi and all the other southern states. On sweltering summer days and crisp autumn mornings I have looked at her beautiful churches with their spires pointing heavenward. I have beheld the impressive outlay of her massive religious education buildings. Over and over again I have found myself asking: "Who worships here? Who is their God? [109] Where were their voices when the lips of Governor Barnett[110] dripped with words of interposition and nullification?[111] Where were they when Governor Wallace gave the clarion call for defiance and hatred? [112] Where were their voices of support when tired, bruised, and weary Negro men and women decided to rise from the dark dungeons of complacency to the bright hills of creative protest?"

[109] "Who is their God?" is not a question found in the Bible but a question of Dr. King asked to the complacent white churches of his day. However, the Scriptures do give us an extensive answer to the question, "Who is God?" The Bible tells us a great deal about who God is for those who believe the Scriptures. A few examples from the first books of the Old Testament give us the beginnings of a "theology" or words about God that come from God's Word:

> (Genesis 15:1) Do not be afraid, Abram. I am your shield, your very great reward.

> (Genesis 18:25) Will not the Judge of all the earth do right?

> (Exodus 34:5-7) Then the LORD came down in the cloud and stood there with him and proclaimed his name, the LORD. {6} And he passed in front of Moses, proclaiming, "The LORD, the LORD, the compassionate and gracious God, slow to anger, abounding in love and faithfulness, {7} maintaining love to thousands, and forgiving wickedness, rebellion and sin. Yet he does not leave the guilty unpunished; he punishes the children and their children for the sin of the fathers to the third and fourth generation."

> (Numbers 23:19) God is not a man, that he should lie, nor a son of man, that he should change his mind. Does he speak and then not act? Does he promise and not fulfill?

> (Deuteronomy 3:24) "O Sovereign LORD, you have begun to show to your servant your greatness and your strong hand. For what god is there in heaven or on earth who can do the deeds and mighty works you do?

> (Deuteronomy 4:24) For the LORD your God is a consuming fire, a jealous God.

> (Deuteronomy 4:31) For the LORD your God is

a merciful God; he will not abandon or destroy
you or forget the covenant with your forefathers,
which he confirmed to them by oath.

(Deuteronomy 6:4 NIV) Hear, O Israel: The
LORD our God, the LORD is one.

(Deuteronomy 10:17) For the LORD your God
is God of gods and Lord of lords, the great God,
mighty and awesome, who shows no partiality
and accepts no bribes.

(Deuteronomy 20:1) When you go to war
against your enemies and see horses and
chariots and an army greater than yours,
do not be afraid of them, because the LORD
your God, who brought you up out of Egypt,
will be with you.

(Deuteronomy 20:4) For the LORD your God
is the one who goes with you to fight for you
against your enemies to give you victory."

A great God gives mere mortals and humble minorities the
courage to do great things.

[110] From 1960 to 1964, Ross Robert Barnett (1898 –1987) was the
Democratic governor of Mississippi. As a segregationist, he resisted
James Meredith's efforts to integrate his alma mater, the University
of Mississippi. Barnett's explicit racist commitments led him to
oppose federal law resulting in conflict with US authorities.

[111] "Interposition and nullification" were two words that defined the
clash between the enforcement of federal law and state law during
the civil rights struggle. To interpose means to stand between so
one forceful entity cannot effect another entity. State leaders sought
to use their local authorities to stand between the federal civil rights
laws that were being enforced after the Supreme Court's decisions.
The word nullification refers to the states' rights claim that the
individual states of the United States could make void a federal law
within their jurisdiction since each state is a sovereign State that
forms the Union. As a result of this view, the States have the final
authority over their own affairs, even with respect to the Federal
Government's efforts to impose national laws on the State's internal

activities. The State's rights defense was a pivotal issue in the Civil War as well as in the civil rights movement in the 1960s.

[112] Martin Luther King, Jr. described Alabama Governor George Wallace (1919-1998) as one the most dangerous racists in America. In his 1963 inaugural address, Wallace pledged "Segregation now! Segregation tomorrow! Segregation forever!" He put his segregationist beliefs into practice when he stood at the entry of the University of Alabama to protest the matriculation of two African American students. In 1963 he called out the Alabama National Guard to prevent the desegregation of Birmingham schools. In 1965, during the Selma to Montgomery March, he overlooked the use of violence. Wallace served four terms as governor during 1963 and 1987.

V.
C. The Church, the Body of Christ, Is Silently Weak & Is Blemished & Scarred Due to Social Neglect.
1. There can be no deep disappointment where there is not deep love. Yes, I love the church.

Yes, these questions are still in my mind. In deep disappointment, I have wept over the laxity of the church. But be assured that my tears have been tears of love. There can be no deep disappointment where there is not deep love. Yes, I love the Church; I love her sacred walls. How could I do otherwise? I am in the rather unique position of being the son, the grandson, and the great-grandson of preachers. Yes, I see the Church as the body of Christ. [113] But, oh! How we have blemished and scarred that body through social neglect and fear of being nonconformist. [114]

[113] The body of Christ as a metaphor for the Church is a central teaching of Paul. In 1 Corinthians 12:12-27 Paul writes, "The body is a unit, though it is made up of many parts; and though all its parts are many, they form one body. So it is with Christ. For we were all baptized by one Spirit into one body—whether Jews or Greeks, slave or free—and we were all given the one Spirit to drink. Now the body is not made up of one part but of many. If the foot should say, 'Because I am not a hand, I do not belong to the body,' it would not for that reason cease to be part of the body. And if the ear should say, 'Because I am not an eye, I do not belong to the body,' it would not for that reason cease to be part of the body. If

the whole body were an eye, where would the sense of hearing be? If the whole body were an ear, where would the sense of smell be? But in fact God has arranged the parts in the body, every one of them, just as he wanted them to be. If they were all one part, where would the body be? As it is, there are many parts, but one body. The eye cannot say to the hand, 'I don't need you!' And the head cannot say to the feet, 'I don't need you!' On the contrary, those parts of the body that seem to be weaker are indispensable, and the parts that we think are less honorable we treat with special honor. And the parts are unpresentable are treated with special modesty, while our presentable parts need no special treatment. But God has combined the members of the body and has given greater honor to the parts that lacked it, so that there should be no division in the body, but that its parts should have equal concern for each other. If one part suffers, every part suffers with it; if one part is honored, every part rejoices with it. Now you are the body of Christ, and each one of you is a part of it." This concept of the unity of all believers in Christ as understood by Dr. King meant that white believers should hurt with their black brothers under the weight of injustice and support their efforts to find justice through nonviolent means.

[114] The fear of being a nonconformist is not just a cultural matter. It also raises a biblical concept as well. Romans 12:1-2 presents Paul's call for Christian "nonconformity" to the world's way of doing things. Romans 12:1-2 says, "Therefore, I urge you, brothers, in view of God's mercy, to offer your bodies as living sacrifices, holy and pleasing to God—this is your spiritual act of worship. Do not conform any longer to the pattern of this world, but be transformed by the renewing of your mind. Then you will be able to test and approve what God's will is—his good, pleasing and perfect will."

2. The Early Church Was Powerful, When It Rejoiced at Being Deemed Worthy to Suffer for Their Beliefs.

There was a time when the Church was very powerful. It was during that period when the early Christians rejoiced when they were deemed worthy to suffer for what they believed. [115] In those days the Church was not merely a thermometer that recorded the ideas and principles of popular opinion; it was a thermostat that transformed the mores of society. Wherever the early Christians entered a town the power structure got disturbed and immediately sought to convict them for being "disturbers of the peace" and "outside agitators." [116] But they went on with the conviction that they were "a colony of heaven"[117] and had to obey God rather than man. [118] They were small in number but big in commitment. They were too God-intoxicated[119] to be "astronomically intimidated." [120] They brought an end to such ancient evils as infanticide and gladiatorial contest. [121]

[115] Here Dr. King refers to the experience of the early church in Acts 5:29, 33-34, 38-42, "Peter and the other apostles replied: 'We must obey God rather than men!'...When they heard this they [the Sanhedrin, the Jewish supreme legal counsel] were furious and wanted to put them to death But a Pharisee named Gamaliel, a teacher of the law, who was honored by all the people, stood up in the Sanhedrin and ordered that the men be put outside for a little while... 'Therefore, in the present case I advise you: Leave these men alone! Let them go! For if their purpose; or activity is of human origin, it will fail. But if it is from God, you will not be able to stop these men; you will only find yourselves fighting against God.' His speech persuaded them. They called the apostles in and had them flogged. Then they ordered them not to speak in the name of Jesus, and let them go. The apostles left the Sanhedrin, rejoicing because they had been counted worthy of suffering disgrace for the Name. Day after day, in the temple courts and from house to house, they never stopped teaching and proclaiming the good news that Jesus is the Christ."

Rejoicing in persecution is rooted in Jesus' teaching in His Beatitudes found in the Sermon on the Mount in Matthew 5:10-13, "Blessed are those who are persecuted because of righteousness, for theirs is the kingdom of heaven. Blessed are you when people insult you, persecute you and falsely say all kinds of evil against you because of me. Rejoice and be glad, because great is your reward in heaven, for in the same way they persecuted the prophets who were before you. You are the salt of the earth. But if the salt loses its saltiness, how can it be made salty again? It is no longer good for anything, except to be thrown out and trampled by men."

[116] Dr. King's phrases in quotes, "disturbers of the peace" and "outside agitators" are not found in the Bible, but are names that were hurled against the civil rights leaders. Significantly, however, similar epithets were slung against the early apostles as seen, for example, in the city of Thessalonica in Acts 17. Acts 17:1, 5-8 relates, "...they came to Thessalonica..."and the ones who"...believed not, moved with envy...gathered a company, and set all the city on an uproar, and assaulted the house of Jason, and sought to bring them out to the people. And when they found them [the apostles] not, they

drew Jason and certain brethren unto the rulers of the city, crying, These that have turned the world upside down are come hither also…and these all do contrary to the decrees of Caesar, saying that there is another king, one Jesus. And they troubled the people and the rulers of the city, when they heard these things." (KJV). Here Dr. King is implying that the civil rights movement experienced the same type of maltreatment as the early Christian missionaries who were under Paul's leadership.

[117] Dr. King's phrase, "A colony of heaven" turns our attention to Philippians 3:20. Paul writes there, "But our citizenship is in heaven. And we eagerly await a Savior from there, the Lord Jesus Christ." The KJV says, "For our conversation is in heaven; from whence also we look for the Saviour, the Lord Jesus Christ." But Dr. King here follows Moffat's translation that reads, "We are a colony of heaven." The Church's citizenship is in heaven.

A colony is a settlement established by citizens living outside their home land, but who continue to be ruled by their mother country and reflect their home land's culture, values and language. The Church is a colony of citizens who live outside their home land of heaven, and so should reflect heaven's culture, values and language. Similarly, in Ephesians 2:19, Paul teaches that when the Ephesians believed in Jesus Christ, they were "no longer strangers and foreigners, but fellow citizens with the saints."

[118] Here Dr. King cites Acts 5:29, "Peter and the other apostles replied:

> 'We must obey God rather than men!'" This text is the core theological reference that warrants civil disobedience for Christians in those circumstances when the law of man requires one to violate the law of God. See note 114 above.

[119] The phrase "God intoxicated" has been applied in various ways. Here Dr. King uses it to describe the complete commitment of early Christians to their faith in Christ regardless of the cost. It has been used to describe the Jewish Enlightenment philosopher Baruch Spinoza (1632-1677). In terms of an official religious use, it can also have direct reference to Sufism, a sub-branch of Islam. According to Sufi philosophy, a *"mast"* (pronounced "must") is a believer who is overpowered by love for God. This condition is marked by a disorientation to a person's environment that parallels intoxication. The Sufi phrase "Mast-Allah" means "intoxicated with God."

[120] The phrase "astronomically Intimidated" suggests a feat that is so

great it cannot be measured. Astronomy measures in light years and thus greater than human experience can comprehend. This phrase as well as other important themes found in the *Letter From Birmingham Jail* come from Dr. King's sermon entitled, "Transformed Nonconformist" dated November 1954. In that sermon he uses the phrase, "We are a colony of heaven, (see note 117) Philippians 3:20 and references Romans 12:2. This sermon was preached shortly after being installed as Dexter Avenue Baptist Church's twentieth pastor in Montgomery, Alabama. He draws on James E. Wall's sermon entitled, "Men who Live Differently", a copy of which he filed in the same folder. Walls was assistant pastor of the Evangelical United Brethren Church in Aurora, Illinois and preached his sermon on May 27, 1951.

Dr. King observes,

> "I have seen many white people who sincerely oppose segregation and discrimination but that never took a real stand against it because of fear of standing alone."
> And be not conformed to this world but be ye transformed by the renewing of your mind. Romans 12:2
> "We are a colony of heaven " Philippians 3:20 [We must not be "astronomically intimidated"]"

He goes on to write,

> Both of these passages suggest that every true Christian is a citizen of two worlds, the world of time and the world of eternity. The Christian finds himself in the paradoxical situation of having to be in the world yet not of the world. Indeed this is what is meant by one of the passages just read in which Christians are referred to as a colony of heaven. This figure of speech should have special relevance for us in America since the early days of our nation's history were days of colonialism. Thirteen of the states of our union were originally British colonies. Although our forefathers had relative freedom in forming their institutions and systems of law their ultimate allegiance was to the King of England. And so although the

> Christian finds himself in the colony of time his
> ultimate allegiance is to the empire of eternity.
> In other words the Christian owes his ultimate
> allegiance to God and if any earthly institution
> conflicts with God's will it is the Christian duty to
> revolt against it. (*Papers*, p. 195.)

[121] Written evidence of the life and death battles of Roman gladiators can be dated to 264 BC, when at the funeral of Junius Brutus, three teams of two fought to the death. With the ascendancy of Christianity in the 300's AD, gladiatorial combat died out. Similarly, the Roman Empire was well acquainted with the practice of infanticide. A father made the decision whether an infant would live or die after birth. Deformed infants were usually left outside at an exposure wall to succumb to the elements. Christians not only did not practice infanticide, but in many instances, they took the infants abandoned to death and raised them in their homes. Accordingly, over time, the early Christian pro-life commitment led to the death of infanticide. Dr. King's point is that Christians from earliest times have stood against cultural and social evils in the name of Christ. His own commitment as well as that of the civil rights movement was a similar attempt to pursue justice by ending segregation. Thus the civil rights cause was a continuation of the ancient Christian Church's pursuit of justice.

3. So Often the Contemporary Church Is a Weak, Ineffectual Voice with an Uncertain Sound.

Things are different now. The contemporary Church is so often a weak, ineffectual voice with an uncertain sound. [122] It is so often the arch-supporter of the status quo. Far from being disturbed by the presence of the Church, the power structure of the average community is consoled by the Church's silent and often vocal sanction of things as they are.

[122] This image is taken from Paul in 1 Corinthians 14:7-8, "Even in the case of lifeless things that make sounds, such as the flute or harp, how will anyone know what tune is being played unless there is a distinction in the notes? Again, if the trumpet does not sound a clear call, who will get ready for battle?"

V.

D. Under God's Judgment, Will the Church Recapture Her Sacrificial Spirit Or Become Irrelevant?

But the judgment of God is upon the Church as never before. [123] If the Church of today does not recapture the sacrificial spirit of the early Church, it will lose its authentic ring, forfeit the loyalty of millions, and be dismissed as an irrelevant social club with no meaning for the twentieth century. I am meeting young people every day whose disappointment with the Church has risen to outright disgust. [124]

[123] Dr. King's teaching that judgment by God begins with judgment on the Church and is coupled with suffering is found in 1 Peter 4:15-19, "If you suffer, it should not be as a murderer or thief or any other kind of criminal, or even as a meddler. However, if you suffer as a Christian, do not be ashamed, but praise God that you bear that name. For it is time for judgment to begin with the family of God; and if it begins with us, what will the outcome be for those who do not obey the gospel of God? And, 'If it is hard for the righteous to be saved, what will become of the ungodly and the sinner?' So then, those who suffer according to God's will should commit themselves to their faithful Creator and continue to do good."

[124] Dr. King's concern for the loss of the younger generation's participation in the life of the Church has not abated over the decades since he wrote his *Letter*. A 2010 front-page story in *USA Today* entitled, "Survey: 72% of Millennials 'more spiritual than religious'" offers data to support this reality. (A "millennial" is a young adult from the generation that came of age around the turn of the new millennium.) According to the data secured by LifeWay Christian Resources, a large majority of 18-to-29-year-olds are "more spiritual than religious." The study found 65% of Millennials who call themselves Christian are Christian in name only; 65% of Millennials rarely or never pray with others; 65% rarely or never attend worship services; 67% don't read the Bible or sacred texts. Similar conclusions were reached by the Pew Forum on Religion & Public Life. Their study, "Religion in the Millennial Generation", discovered that compared to previous generations, fewer Millennials attend worship services or identify with religious communities. Yet other findings suggest that they are acutally similar to the Baby-Boomers: 40% of Millennials say that religion is important in their lives (compared to 39% of Boomers at the same ages); 41% of Millennials pray daily (similar to the 42% of Gen Xers

as young adults); 53% are "certain God exists" (compared to 55% of Gen Xers). Christian Smith, in *Souls in Transition: The Religious and Spiritual Lives of Emerging Adults*, (2009), also provides data on the religious life of 18 to 23 year olds. His research seems to indicate that young adults from conservative religious backgrounds continue to believe and practice their faith, while young adults from the more liberal mainline traditions do not.

V.

E. The Church Is to Be a Witness to the Gospel in Troubled Times. In This Decisive Hour Will The True Church Break the Status Quo, in the Hope That Right Defeated Is Stronger Than Evil Triumphant?

Maybe again I have been too optimistic. Is organized religion too inextricably bound to the status quo to save our nation and the world? Maybe I must turn my faith to the inner spiritual Church, the church within the Church, as the true ecclesia[125] and the hope of the world. [126] But again I am thankful to God that some noble souls from the ranks of organized religion have broken loose from the paralyzing chains of conformity and joined us as active partners in the struggle for freedom. They have left their secure congregations and walked the streets of Albany, Georgia, [127] with us. They have gone through the highways of the South on torturous rides for freedom. Yes, they have gone to jail with us. Some have been kicked out of their churches and lost the support of their bishops and fellow ministers. But they have gone with the faith that right defeated is stronger than evil triumphant. [128] These men have been the leaven in the lump of the race. [129]Their witness has been the spiritual salt that has preserved the true meaning of the Gospel[130] in these troubled times. They have carved a tunnel of hope through the dark mountain of disappointment.

[125] *Ecclesia* or "*Ekklesia*" are the Latin and Greek words for Church that are often left untranslated when used in English theological discussions. The concept of the *Ekklesia* can refer either to a local organized church in a specific area, such as First Presbyterian Church of Birmingham, or Dexter Avenue Baptist Church of Montgomery, or to the spiritual body of the Church that is composed of all the believers in all places from all times considered as a whole. Here Dr. King has the latter in mind. This inner spiritual body composed of all true believers that creates the true body of the Christian Church is sometimes called the invisible church, the

universal Church or the holy catholic church. Dr. King's frustration with visible local churches is met by his affirmation that he still is committed to the church even if he can only find true spirituality in the invisible church.

[126] Dr. King speaks here of the "hope of the world". Hope is the sure expectation of that which is yet future. The sure expectation in the Bible is because of God's gracious and powerful nature that enables Him to keep His promises to His people. Hope is a sure part of the spiritual inner church because it is inseparably tied to God's love in Christ. This is why even when things are hard in a believer's life in this world, the believer always has hope to carry him on. Hope is used around 130 to 170 times in the Bible depending on the translation. As an example of the Bible's teaching on hope, consider these texts from Paul's letter to the Romans from the KJV:

> Romans 4:18
> Who (Abram) against hope believed in hope, that he might become the father of many nations, according to that which was spoken, 'So shall thy seed be.'

> Romans 5:2
> By whom also we have access by faith into this grace wherein we stand, and rejoice in hope of the glory of God.

> Romans 5:4-5
> And patience, experience; and experience, hope: And hope maketh not ashamed; because the love of God is shed abroad in our hearts by the Holy Ghost which is given unto us.
> Romans 8:20
> For the creature was made subject to vanity, not willingly, but by reason of him who hath subjected the same in hope,

> Romans 8:24-25
> For we are saved by hope: but hope that is seen is not hope: for what a man seeth, why doth he yet hope for? But if we hope for that we see not, then do we with patience wait for it.

Romans 12:12
Rejoicing in hope; patient in tribulation; continuing instant in prayer;

Romans 15:4
For whatsoever things were written aforetime were written for our learning, that we through patience and comfort of the scriptures might have hope.

Romans 15:13
Now the God of hope fill you with all joy and peace in believing, that ye may abound in hope, through the power of the Holy Ghost.

[127] The Albany Movement was established in 1961 by various civil rights organizations. It led an effort to address segregation and discrimination in all forms. Martin Luther King, Jr. and the Southern Christian Leadership Conference (SCLC) joined the effort in December 1961, bringing nationwide attention to Albany. It achieved few advances because of the jailing of hundreds of protesters. After his second arrest, Dr. King agreed in August 1962 to leave Albany and end the demonstrations. Dr. King believed the lack of success of the Albany campaign was due to its too broad of scope. From lessons learned in Albany, Dr. King was better able to shape his plans for the Birmingham Campaign of 1963.

[128] "Right defeated is stronger than evil triumphant." This optimism in justice even when its efforts are unsuccessful flows from the commitment of love to overcome evil with good, and the recognition that the discouraging defeat of the cross leads to the triumphant joy of the resurrection. A historic Christian saying declares, there is no crown without the cross. Romans 12:9-21 teaches, "Love must be sincere. Hate what is evil; cling to what is good. Be devoted to one another in brotherly love. Honor one another above yourselves. Never be lacking in zeal, but keep your spiritual fervor, serving the Lord. Be joyful in hope, patient in affliction, faithful in prayer. Share with God's people who are in need. Practice hospitality. Bless those who persecute you; bless and do not curse. Rejoice with those who rejoice; mourn with those who mourn. Live in harmony with one another. Do not be proud, but be willing to associate with people of low position. Do not be conceited. Do not repay anyone evil for evil. Be careful to do what is right in the eyes of everybody. If it is

possible, as far as it depends on you, live at peace with everyone. Do not take revenge, my friends, but leave room for God's wrath, for it is written: "It is mine to avenge; I will repay, says the Lord. On the contrary: 'If your enemy is hungry, feed him; if he is thirsty, give him something to drink. In doing this, you will heap burning coals on his head.' Do not be overcome by evil, but overcome evil with good." 1 Corinthians 15:58 reflects this resurrection optimism, "Therefore, my dear brothers, stand firm. Let nothing move you. Always give yourselves fully to the work of the Lord, because you know that your labor in the Lord is not in vain." Dr. King's sense of optimism seen in the white supporters who joined the civil rights cause often at great personal risk and cost to themselves practiced a form of optimism that he describes in the memorable line, "They have carved a tunnel of hope through the dark mountain of disappointment."

[129] "Leaven in the lump" is a biblical Old Testament and New Testament metaphor. In the Scriptures, leaven can represent that which is evil as well as that which is good. When leaven represents evil it stands for an outside influence that diminishes something's purity. Thus leaven was prohibited from the Old Testament sacrifices (Leviticus 2:11; 6:16) and the Passover bread (Exodus 12:14-20), which was literally called "unleavened bread". It is used in this negative sense when Jesus speaks of the teaching and hypocrisy of the Pharisees as "the leaven of the Pharisees" (Matthew 16:6; Luke 12:1). Paul speaks of removing a sinful brother from the Christian fellowship as akin to the Old Testament process of removing leaven from the house in preparation for the Passover meal (1 Corinthians 5:6-13). The danger of leaven is that it eventually impacts all of the dough. Thus Paul writes In Galatians 5:9, "A little yeast works through the whole batch of dough." Nevertheless, leaven is also used by Jesus as a positive force precisely because of its ability to permeate and influence an entire lump of dough for good as the dough is being prepared for the baking of normal bread. Matthew 13:33 says, "He told them still another parable: 'The kingdom of heaven is like yeast that a woman took and mixed into a large amount of flour until it worked all through the dough.'" It is in this sense that Dr. King is using the image of leaven. The small number of white anti-segregationists in the South, although looked at as unclean by the segregationist South, was actually a force for good. This powerful force for good would ultimately impact the entire South by the growth of their principles and the influence of their lives. Thus they are "the leaven in the lump of the race". [130] The "true meaning of the Gospel" Dr. King says is "preserved" by

"spiritual salt". This is a reference to Matthew 5:13, "You are the salt of the earth. But if the salt loses its saltiness, how can it be made salty again? It is no longer good for anything, except to be thrown out and trampled by men." See notes 107 and 114 above.

VI. A Note of Hope in God's Will for American Freedom: No Despair for the Future, Because the Will of God and the Sacred Heritage of America Is Freedom.

I hope the Church as a whole will meet the challenge of this decisive hour. But even if the Church does not come to the aid of justice, I have no despair about the future. I have no fear about the outcome of our struggle in Birmingham, even if our motives are presently misunderstood. We will reach the goal of freedom in Birmingham and all over the nation, because the goal of America is freedom. [131] Abused and scorned though we may be, our destiny is tied up with the destiny of America. Before the pilgrims landed at Plymouth, we were here. [132] Before the pen of Jefferson etched across the pages of history the majestic words of the Declaration of Independence, we were here. [133] For more than two centuries our foreparents labored in this country without wages[134]; they made cotton "king";[135] and they built the homes of their masters in the midst of brutal injustice and shameful humiliation -- and yet out of a bottomless vitality they continued to thrive and develop. If the inexpressible cruelties of slavery could not stop us, the opposition we now face will surely fail. We will win our freedom because the sacred heritage of our nation[136] and the eternal will of God[137] are embodied in our echoing demands.

[131] The "goal of America is freedom." This great end of the American experiment expressed by Dr. King is consistent with the words of President George Washington spoken at his First Inaugural Address, on April 30, 1789, "The preservation of the sacred fire of liberty and the destiny of the republican model of government are justly considered as deeply, perhaps as finally, staked on the experiment entrusted to the hands of the American people."

[132] Dr. King's history is correct. The English Jamestown settlement in Virginia was established in 1607. The first Africans to arrive at this earliest English colony in America probably landed in 1619. They were brought to Jamestown as indentured servants by a Dutch ship. The pilgrims arrived at Plymouth Rock in Massachusetts the following year in 1620.

[133] Since the Africans arrived in the New World in 1619, they had been there for more than 150 years when Thomas Jefferson wrote the Declaration of Independence. In fact, Jefferson's draft of the Declaration actually called for the ending of slavery. But this was edited out of the Declaration by the Continental Congress since this was not the unanimous view of the delegates. Jefferson's unedited text states as he enumerates the injustices of the King of England,

> ...he has waged cruel war against human nature itself, violating its most sacred rights of life & liberty in the persons of a distant people who never offended him, captivating & carrying them into slavery in another hemisphere, or to incur miserable death in their transportation thither. This piratical warfare, the opprobrium of *infidel* powers, is the warfare of the CHRISTIAN king of Great Britain. determined to keep open a market where MEN should be bought & sold, he has prostituted his negative for suppressing every legislative attempt to prohibit or to restrain this execrable commerce: and that this assemblage of horrors might want no fact of distinguished die, he is now exciting those very people to rise in arms among us, and to purchase that liberty of which *he* has deprived them, by murdering the people upon whom *he* also obtruded them; thus paying off former crimes committed against the *liberties* of one people, with crimes which he urges them to commit against the *lives* of another.

[134] Dr. King refers to two centuries of slave labor in the English colonies without wages. Lincoln's Second Inaugural Address in the throes of the Civil War refers to this as well with his poignant words,

> One-eighth of the whole population were colored slaves, not distributed generally over the Union, but localized in the southern part of it. These slaves constituted a peculiar and powerful interest. All knew that this interest was somehow the cause of the war. To strengthen, perpetuate, and extend this interest was the object for which the insurgents would rend the Union even by war,

while the Government claimed no right to do more than to restrict the territorial enlargement of it. Neither party expected for the war the magnitude or the duration which it has already attained. Neither anticipated that the *cause* of the conflict might cease with or even before the conflict itself should cease. Each looked for an easier triumph, and a result less fundamental and astounding. Both read the same Bible and pray to the same God, and each invokes His aid against the other. It may seem strange that any men should dare to ask a just God's assistance in wringing their bread from the sweat of other men's faces, but let us judge not, that we be not judged. The prayers of both could not be answered. That of neither has been answered fully. The Almighty has His own purposes. "Woe unto the world because of offenses; for it must needs be that offenses come, but woe to that man by whom the offense cometh." If we shall suppose that American slavery is one of those offenses which, in the providence of God, must needs come, but which, having continued through His appointed time, He now wills to remove, and that He gives to both North and South this terrible war as the woe due to those by whom the offense came, shall we discern therein any departure from those divine attributes which the believers in a living God always ascribe to Him? Fondly do we hope, fervently do we pray, that this mighty scourge of war may speedily pass away. Yet, if God wills that it continue until all the wealth piled by the bondsman's two hundred and fifty years of unrequited toil shall be sunk, and until every drop of blood drawn with the lash shall be paid by another drawn with the sword, as was said three thousand years ago, so still it must be said "the judgments of the Lord are true and righteous altogether."

[135] "They made cotton king." The extraordinary growth of the southern cotton market in the years leading up to the Civil War

was made possible by the labor of southern slaves and advances in technology during the industrial revolution. The importance of the South's supply of cotton to the world was undisputed. Thus "King Cotton" became the international policy of the Confederate States diplomats in the Civil War. But the South's refusal to ship cotton to European markets with the purpose of forcing European countries to intervene in the American Civil War failed. Instead, the British opened up new sources of cotton production in other countries, and the European countries remained uninvolved in the war. With the Union's blockade of Southern ports, no cotton could be exported which meant that cotton was no longer king. Perhaps with poetic justice, the wealth acquired through cotton and slaves was not able to be used to defend the slave holding states in the war.

[136] "Freedom" and "the sacred heritage of our nation" are closely related in Dr. King's understanding. Freedom and the sacred or the holy are interconnected, for example, in his Historic "I Have a Dream" speech. Note how is this short example how closely faith and Scripture are linked with the dream of freedom (Scripture quotations or allusions are underlined, faith words are put in bold):

> I have a *dream* today!
>
> I have a dream that one day every valley shall be exalted, and every hill and mountain shall be made low, the rough places will be made plain, and the crooked places will be made straight; "and the glory of the Lord shall be revealed and all flesh shall see it together." [The underlined words are from the Biblical passage of Isaiah 40:4-5.]
>
> This is our hope, and this is the faith that I go back to the South with.
>
> With this faith, we will be able to hew out of the mountain of despair a stone of hope. With this faith, we will be able to transform the jangling discords of our nation into a beautiful symphony of brotherhood. With this faith, we will be able to work together, to pray together, to struggle together, to go to jail together, to stand up for freedom together, knowing that we will be free one day.
>
> And this will be the day -- this will be the day when all of God's children will be able to sing with new meaning:

> My country 'tis of thee, sweet land of liberty, of thee I sing.
> Land where my fathers died, land of the Pilgrim's pride,
> From every mountainside, let freedom ring!
> And if America is to be a great nation, this must become true.

[137] "The eternal will of God" is linked with freedom in Dr. King's mind. This is an inference that he draws from Biblical teachings such as: Leviticus 25:10, "Proclaim liberty throughout the land unto all the inhabitants thereof" (KJV, which is the verse on the Liberty Bell); Luke 4:14-21, "Jesus returned to Galilee in the power of the Spirit.... The scroll of the prophet Isaiah was handed to him. Unrolling it, he found the place where it is written: 'The Spirit of the Lord is on me, because he has anointed me to preach good news to the poor. He has sent me to proclaim freedom for the prisoners and recovery of sight for the blind to release the oppressed, to proclaim the year of the Lord's favor...'and he began by saying to them, 'Today this scripture is fulfilled in your hearing.'"; John 8:32, 36, "Then you will know the truth, and the truth will set you free....So if the Son sets you free, you will be free indeed."; 2 Corinthians 3:17, "Now the Lord is the Spirit, and where the Spirit of the Lord is, there is freedom."

VII. Who Are the True Heroes: Birmingham's Policemen Or the Nonviolent Demonstrators?
A. It Is Wrong: To Do the Right Deed for the Wrong Reason, Or To Do the Wrong Deed for the Right Reason. (Both Are Wrong: To Use Immoral Means to Attain Moral Ends Or To Use Moral Means to Attain Immoral Ends.)
1. The Commendation of Policemen Is Inappropriate in View of the Inhumane Treatment of Negroes in Jail.

I must close now. But before closing I am impelled to mention one other point in your statement that troubled me profoundly. You warmly commend the Birmingham police force for keeping "order" and "preventing violence." I don't believe you would have so warmly commended the police force[138] if you had seen its angry violent dogs literally biting six unarmed, nonviolent Negroes. I don't believe you would so quickly commend the policemen if you would observe their ugly and inhuman treatment of Negroes here in the city jail; if you would watch them push and curse old Negro women and young Negro girls; if you would see them slap and kick old Negro men and young Negro boys; if you will observe them, as they did on two occasions, refuse to give us food because we wanted to sing our grace together. I'm sorry that I can't join you in your praise for the police department.

> [138] Under the leadership of Eugene Bull Connor, the Birmingham police, responded with power and cruelty. They condoned civil rights violations and KKK activities. In 1963, the police Commissioner Connor ordered the use of fire hoses and dogs to stop the demonstrators. These images were carried on national television prompting protests all across the country.

2. Even If the Police Behaved Nonviolently, Still Their Purpose Was to Preserve the Evils Segregation.

It is true that they have been rather disciplined in their public handling of the demonstrators. In this sense they have been rather publicly "nonviolent." But for what purpose? To preserve the evil system of segregation. Over the last few years I have consistently preached that nonviolence demands the means we use must be as pure as the ends we seek. So I have tried to make it clear that it is wrong to use immoral means to attain moral ends.[139] But now I must affirm that it is just as wrong or even more so to use moral means to preserve immoral ends.[140] Maybe Mr. Connor and his policemen have been rather publicly nonviolent, as Chief Pritchett[141] was in Albany, Georgia, but they have used the moral means of nonviolence to maintain the immoral end of flagrant injustice. T. S. Eliot has said that there is no greater treason than to do the right deed for the wrong reason.[142]

> [139] Here Dr. King's ethic for social change stands in stark contrast to that advocated by another 20th Century social change activist, Saul Alinsky. Dr. King writes, "Over the last few years I have consistently preached that nonviolence demands the means we use must be as pure as the ends we seek. So I have tried to make it clear that it is wrong to use immoral means to attain moral ends. But now I must affirm that it is just as wrong or even more so to use moral means to preserve immoral ends." Compare this with Alinsky's perspective on "means" and "ends" as seen in his *Rules for Radicals*. (Saul D. Alinsky, *Rules For Radicals: A Pragmatic Primer for Realistic Radicals* (New York: Vintage Books, 1989)). Alinsky's socialist thought has been seen by many as an American application of Marx's call for

revolution to create economic change.

[140] Basic questions of ethics include the use of just means for unjust ends and unjust means for a just end. Does the end justify the means? Do the means justify the end? Dr. King would argue that both are wrong. If killing an innocent person brings about peace does that make it right to kill? If non-violent police officers effectively uphold the law but the law that they are upholding is segregation, does the police good behavior make the segregation laws just? Dr. King was willing to recognize that the police may have done their jobs well in many cases, but their good use of means did not make the evil end a good end.

[141] Laurie Pritchett was Chief of police in Albany, Georgia from 1959 to 1966. He successfully resisted the efforts of the Albany protestors in 1961 through his careful planning and nonviolent law enforcement. Pritchett had made arrangements with local city jails for the possible arrests. He insisted that the law be enforced without violence in defense of the public order, without appeal to the racially destabilizing segregation laws. Without the outbreak of violence little media coverage was given to the Albany protests.

[142] The exact quote of T. S. Eliot is given by Dr. King in the final version. It states, "The last temptation is the greatest treason: To do the right deed for the wrong reason." Thomas Stearns Eliot, or T. S. Eliot, was born in 1888 and died in 1965. He received the Nobel Prize in Literature in 1948. Dr. King's quotation of Eliot is from *Murder in The Cathedral*, Eliot's 1935 drama that presents the assassination of Archbishop Thomas Becket in Canterbury Cathedral in 1170. The theme of the play highlights opposition to authority. Given that 1935 was in the era of the emerging dictatorships of Europe in the decade before WWII, it has been interpreted as a call for opposition to the Nazi assaults against historic Christian values. In the scene from which Dr. King quotes, Archbishop Thomas Becket is offered martyrdom. While this is refused, Becket recognizes that his untimely death is certain. The dramatic verse declares:

> Now is my way clear, now is the meaning plain:
> Temptation shall not come in this kind again.
> The last temptation is the greatest treason:
> To do the right deed for the wrong reason.

VII.

B. Nonviolent Protestors in This Just Cause Have Displayed Real Heroism by Their Courage, Suffering and Discipline in the Midst of

Great Provocation: This is the Best of the American Dream, One of the Most Sacred Values in Our Judaeo-Christian Heritage, Thereby Bringing Our Nation Back to The Great Wells of Democracy Which Were Dug Deep by the Founding Fathers.

I wish you had commended the Negro sit-inners and demonstrators of Birmingham for their sublime courage, their willingness to suffer, and their amazing discipline in the midst of the most inhuman provocation. One day the South will recognize its real heroes. They will be the James Merediths[143], courageously and with a majestic sense of purpose, facing jeering and hostile mobs and the agonizing loneliness that characterizes the life of the pioneer. They will be old, oppressed, battered Negro women, symbolized in a seventy-two year old woman of Montgomery, Alabama, who rose up with a sense of dignity and with her people decided not to ride the segregated buses, and responded to one who inquired about her tiredness with ungrammatical profundity: "My feets is tired, but my soul is rested." They will be the young high school and college students, young ministers of the gospel and a host of their elders courageously and nonviolently sitting-in at lunch counters and willingly going to jail for conscience sake.[144] One day the South will know that when these disinherited children of God[145] sat down at lunch counters they were in reality standing up for the best in the American dream and the most sacred values in our Judaeo-Christian heritage[146], and thus carrying our whole nation back to great wells of democracy which were dug deep by the founding fathers[147] in the formulation of the Constitution[148] and the Declaration of Independence[149].

[143] In 1961, James Meredith applied to the segregated University of Mississippi. Although rejected twice, with the aid of the NAACP, he was finally accepted. His admittance in 1962, however, only came after court challenges, opposition from Mississippi Governor Ross Barnett and campus riots that were marked by violence. Meredith ultimately graduated with a degree in political science. His efforts at encouraging black voter registration was met with being wounded by a gunman. He went on to earn a law degree from Columbia University in New York and to run unsuccessfully on various occasions for public office in Mississippi.

[144] Going to jail for conscience sake is a historic reality in the early Christian tradition. Acts 5:18 says, "They arrested the apostles and put them in the public jail." 1 Peter 4:15-16 states, "If you suffer, it should not be as a murderer or thief or any other kind of criminal or even as a meddler. However, if you suffer as a Christian, do not be

ashamed, but praise God that you bear that name." Acts 5:41 notes, "The apostles left the Sanhedrin, rejoicing because they had been counted worthy of suffering disgrace for the Name."

[145] The theological tension in the phrase "disinherited children of God" is palpable. The blacks had been disinherited by the whites of the South through the policy of segregation. Nevertheless, they were still children of God, and thus were entitled to the divine inheritance. God's adoption was holding fast, even while man's rejection and disinheriting was the stated policy. This is an echo of John 1:11-12, "He came unto his own, an dhis own received him not. But as many as received him, to them gave he power to become the sons of God, even to them that believe on his name." (KJV).

[146] Dr. King's "...the most sacred values in our Judaeo-Christian heritage" is an ironic statement since both Christian and Jewish clergymen were the immediate recipients of his *Letter*. The core idea of the Judaeo-Christian heritage is the belief that the one true God has given His people the true revelation of Himself seen especially in the Ten Commandments that define true worship and true justice. The phrase itself does not argue that Judaism and Christianity are the same. Rather, it implies that the core values and beliefs of America emerge from the teachings of the Old Testament prophets and the New Testament teachings of Jesus Christ. These values have created the culture of America that has enabled the great success of American liberty and law which are expressed in the political structures created by the Declaration of Independence and US Constitution. The phrase "Judaeo-Christian" also has been employed to broaden American culture's description of its history. While America began as a largely Protestant and Christian nation, over time it has welcomed the contributions of the Jewish immigrants, and thus the phrase seeks to avoid an implicit or unintended anti-Semitism. Finally, the term has become even more relevant for many as American culture has engaged the twin forces of secularism and atheism and also encountered the hostilities of Islamic *jihad* as manifested in the September 11 terrorist attacks upon the US.

[147] Dr. King's phrase, "...great wells of democracy which were dug deep by the founding fathers" shows his belief that ultimately justice would emerge from the democratic system that the founders initiated. For example, the Declaration of Independence's assertion in 1776 that, "we are endowed by our creator with certain unalienable rights" certainly has direct application to African Americans. But the truth of this deeply dug well of democracy did not become a reality for

African Americans for two more centuries. Thus Dr. King's seeming radicalism in challenging segregation in his mind was grounded in his understanding of the democratic foundations of America. See note 131 above that considers Thomas Jefferson's first draft of the Declaration that included the ending of slavery in America.

[148] Dr. King's phrase, "...their formulation of the Constitution" is simultaneously ironic and accurate. The irony is that the US Constitution began as a compromise between free and slave states. Thus the slave was not given the full dignity of personhood by the Constitution out of deference to both the northern and southern states. For the North, the compromise was reached that a slave was valued at only three fifths of a person that kept the south from having too many people for voting purposes so the southern and northern states were more equally represented in congress. For the South, the compromise was in the simple fact that slavery was allowed to continue. The framers of the Constitution believed that there would have been no Constitution if the compromise over slavery had not been accepted. It took the horrific bloodshed of the Civil War to resolve the issue. Nevertheless, Dr. King's Americanism is clear in that his hope was that the process of desegregation would in effect include the African-American in the opening language of the US Constitution, "WE THE PEOPLE", not as three fifths of a person, not as slaves, not as theoretically freed citizens who had nevertheless been denied their civil rights, but as fully functioning members and citizens of the United States under its Constitutional government exercising and enjoying the full privilege of its Bill of Rights.

[149] See note 146 above for Dr. King's appeal to "the Declaration of Independence".

VIII. Concluding Hopes: No Longer to Be a Civil Rights Leader, But a Clergyman and a Christian Brother, Hoping That Racial Prejudice Will Soon Pass Away.
A. The Fruits of a Narrow Jail Cell: A Long Letter with Long Thoughts and Long Prayers.

Never before have I written a letter this long (or should I say a book?). I'm afraid it is much too long to take your precious time. I can assure you that it would have been much shorter if I had been writing from a comfortable desk, but what else is there to do when you are alone for days in the dull monotony of a narrow jail cell other than write long letters, think strange thoughts, and pray long prayers?

B. Forgiveness Sought If Truth Has Been Overstated Or If Less Than Brotherhood Is In View.

If I have said anything in this letter that is an overstatement of the truth and is indicative of an unreasonable impatience, I beg you to forgive me. If I have said anything in this letter that is an understatement of the truth and is indicative of my having a patience that makes me patient with anything less than brotherhood, I beg God to forgive me.[150]

> [150] Dr. King's words, "settle for anything less than brotherhood, I beg God to forgive me" reflect the core prayer of the Christian faith, the Lord's Prayer. Not only does it begin with the language, "Our Father" which puts all who truly pray it on the ground of a common brotherhood, but it also calls on God to forgive the one who prays even while it insists on the one who prays also forgiving others. Matthew 6:9-13 in the KJV says,
>
> > Our Father which art in heaven,
> > Hallowed be thy name.
> > Thy kingdom come.
> > Thy will be done
> > In earth, as it is in heaven.
> > Give us this day our daily bread.
> > And forgive us our debts,
> > As we forgive our debtors.
> > And lead us not into temptation,
> > But deliver us from evil:
> > For thine is the kingdom,
> > And the Power,
> > And the glory, for ever. Amen.

C. Final Hopes: That the Need for Civil Rights Leadership Will End & Racial Prejudice Will Pass Away.

I hope this letter finds you strong in the faith.[151] I also hope that circumstances will soon make it possible for me to meet each of you, not as an integrationist or a civil rights leader, but as a fellow clergyman and a Christian brother.[152] Let us all hope that the dark clouds of racial prejudice will soon pass away and the deep fog of misunderstanding will be lifted from our fear-drenched communities and in some not too distant tomorrow the radiant stars of love[153] and brotherhood will shine over our great nation with all their scintillating beauty.

Yours for the cause of Peace and Brotherhood,[154]

MARTIN LUTHER KING, JR.

[151] Dr. King's words, "strong in the faith" reflect biblical teaching. 1 Corinthians 16:13 in the KJV says, "Watch ye, stand fast in the faith, quit you like men, be strong."

[152] Dr. King reminds the clergymen who have criticized him by their open letter, that he as the author of this *Letter* to them is also a clergymen and a Christian believer. His phrase "fellow clergyman and a Christian brother" creates a sense of irony as to why he is in jail and they are not since they all together are the same in their clerical vocation.

[153] Dr. King's phrase "the radiant stars of love and brotherhood" may appeal to an image from Paul in Philippians 2:14-16, "Do everything without complaining or arguing, so that you may become blameless and pure, children of God without fault in a crooked and depraved generation, in which you shine like stars in the universe as you hold out the word of life...."

[154] Dr. King's conclusion is again one of irony and integrity. He has been accused of being an outside agitator, yet, he wishes to be known as "Yours for the cause of cause of Peace and Brotherhood". This conclusion is one of integrity because his protest is nonviolent in nature. He wishes to disturb no one's peace and he desires to treat all as brothers. His dream was ever that all could stand together in unity:

> I have a dream today.
>
> I have a dream that one day every valley shall be exalted, every hill and mountain shall be made low, the rough places will be made plain, and the crooked places will be made straight, and the glory of the Lord shall be revealed, and all flesh shall see it together.
>
> This is our hope. This is the faith that I go back to the South with. With this faith we will be able to hew out of the mountain of despair a stone of hope. With this faith we will be able to transform the jangling discords of our nation into a beautiful symphony of brotherhood. With this faith we

will be able to work together, to pray together, to struggle together, to go to jail together, to stand up for freedom together, knowing that we will be free one day.

This will be the day when all of God's children will be able to sing with a new meaning, "My country, 'tis of thee, sweet land of liberty, of thee I sing. Land where my fathers died, land of the pilgrim's pride, from every mountainside, let freedom ring."

And if America is to be a great nation this must become true. So let freedom ring from the prodigious hilltops of New Hampshire. Let freedom ring from the mighty mountains of New York. Let freedom ring from the heightening Alleghenies of Pennsylvania!

Let freedom ring from the snowcapped Rockies of Colorado!

Let freedom ring from the curvaceous slopes of California!

But not only that; let freedom ring from Stone Mountain of Georgia!

Let freedom ring from Lookout Mountain of Tennessee!

Let freedom ring from every hill and molehill of Mississippi. From every mountainside, let freedom ring.

And when this happens, when we allow freedom to ring, when we let it ring from every village and every hamlet, from every state and every city, we will be able to speed up that day when all of God's children, black men and white men, Jews and Gentiles, Protestants and Catholics, will be able to join hands and sing in the words of the old Negro spiritual, "Free at last! free at last! thank God Almighty, we are free at last!"

DR. MARTIN LUTHER KING JR.'S LETTER FROM BIRMINGHAM JAIL

Prepared by Dr. Peter A. Lillback

Activism

You deplore the demonstrations taking place In Birmingham. But your statement, I am sorry to say, fails to express a similar concern for the conditions that brought about the demonstrations. I am sure that none of you would want to rest content with the superficial kind of social analysis that deals merely with effects and does not grapple with underlying causes. p. 2 (II. A.4.)

We must come to see that, as the federal courts have consistently affirmed, it is immoral to urge an individual to withdraw his efforts to gain his basic constitutional rights because the quest precipitates violence. Society must protect the robbed and punish the robber. p. 10 (III. E.)

We will have to repent in this generation not merely for the vitriolic words and actions of the bad people but for the appalling silence of the good people. We must come to see that human progress never rolls in on wheels of inevitability; it comes through the tireless efforts and persistent work of men willing to be co-workers with God, and without this hard work, time itself becomes an ally of the forces of social stagnation. We must use time creatively, and forever realize that the time is always ripe to do right. Now is the time to make real the promise of democracy and transform our pending national elegy into a creative psalm of brotherhood. Now is the time to lift our national policy from the quicksand of racial injustice to the solid rock of human dignity. p. 10 (III. F.)

America's Heritage of Freedom

Oppressed people cannot remain oppressed forever. The urge for freedom will eventually come. This is what has happened to the American Negro.

Something within has reminded him of his birthright of freedom; something without has reminded him that it he can gain it. p. 11 (IV. A)

I hope the church as a whole will meet the challenge of this decisive hour. But even if the church does not come to the aid of justice, I have no despair about the future. I have no fear about the outcome of our struggle in Birmingham, even if our motives are at present misunderstood. We will reach the goal of freedom in Birmingham, and all over the nation, because the goal of America is freedom. Abused and scorned though we may be, our destiny is tied up with America's destiny. Before the pilgrims landed at Plymouth, we were here. Before the pen of Jefferson etched the majestic words of the Declaration of Independence across the pages of history, we were here. p. 17 (VI.)

For more than two centuries our forebears labored in this country without wages; they made cotton king; they built the homes of their masters in the midst of brutal injustice and shameful humiliation-and yet out of a bottomless vitality they continued to thrive and develop. If the inexpressible cruelties of slavery could not stop us, the opposition we now face will surely fail. We will win our freedom because the sacred heritage of our nation and the eternal will of God are embodied in our echoing demands. p. 17 (VI.)

I wish you had commended the Negro sit-inners and demonstrators of Birmingham for their sublime courage, their willingness to suffer and their amazing discipline in the midst of the most inhuman provocation. One day the South will recognize its real heroes…. They will be the young high school and college students, the young ministers of the gospel and a host of their elders, courageously and nonviolently sitting in at lunch counters and willingly going to jail for conscience' sake. One day the South will know that when these disinherited children of God sat down at lunch counters, they were in reality standing up for what is best in the American dream and for the most sacred values in our Judaeo-Christian heritage, thereby bringing our nation back to those great wells of democracy which were dug deep by the founding fathers in their formulation of the Constitution and the Declaration of Independence. p. 18 (VII. B.)

Brotherhood
I hope this letter finds you strong in the faith. I also hope that circumstances will soon make it possible for me to meet each of you, not as an integrationist or a civil rights leader but as a fellow clergyman and a Christian brother.

Let us all hope that the dark clouds of racial prejudice will soon pass away and the deep fog of misunderstanding will be lifted from our fear-drenched communities, and in some not too distant tomorrow the radiant stars of love and brotherhood will shine over our great nation with all their scintillating beauty. p. 19 (VIII. C.)

Church in Society
I felt that the white ministers, priests and rabbis of the South would be among our strongest allies. Instead, some have been outright opponents, refusing to understand the freedom movement and misrepresenting its leaders; all too many others have been more cautious than courageous and have remained silent behind the anesthetizing security of stained-glass windows. p. 14 (V. A. 4.)

In the midst of blatant injustices inflicted upon the Negro, I have watched white churches stand on the sideline and merely mouth pious irrelevancies and sanctimonious trivialities. In the midst of a mighty struggle to rid our nation of racial and economic injustice, I have heard many ministers say: "Those are social issues, with which the gospel has no real concern," and I have watched so many churches commit themselves to a completely other worldly religion which made a strange distinction between body and soul, the sacred and the secular. p. 14 (V. B. 1.)

In deep disappointment I have wept over the laxity of the church. But be assured that my tears have been tears of love. There can be no deep disappointment where there is not deep love. Yes, I love the church; I love her sacred walls. How could I do otherwise? I am in the rather unique position of being the son, the grandson and the great-grandson of preachers. Yes, I see the church as the body of Christ. But, oh! How we have blemished and scarred that body through social neglect and through fear of being nonconformist. p. 15 (V. C. 1.)

There was a time when the church was very powerful, in the time when the early Christians rejoiced at being deemed worthy to suffer for what they believed. In those days the church was not merely a thermometer that recorded the ideas and principles of popular opinion; it was a thermostat that transformed the mores of society. p. 15 (V. C. 2.)

If the Church of today does not recapture the sacrificial spirit of the early church, it will lose its authentic ring, forfeit the loyalty of millions, and be dismissed as an irrelevant social club with no meaning for the twentieth century. I am meeting young people every day whose disappointment with the church has turned into outright disgust. p. 16 (V. D.)

But again I am thankful to God that some noble souls from the ranks of organized religion have broken loose from the paralyzing chains of conformity and joined us as active partners in the struggle for freedom. . . . But they have gone with the faith that right defeated is stronger than evil triumphant...Their witness has been the spiritual salt that has preserved the true meaning of the gospel in these troubled times. They have carved a tunnel of hope through the dark mountain of disappointment. p. 16 (V. E.)

Civil Disobedience

One who breaks an unjust law must do so openly, lovingly, ...and with a willingness to accept the penalty. I submit that an individual who breaks a law that conscience tells him is unjust and who willingly accepts the penalty by staying in jail to arouse the conscience of the community over its injustice, is in reality expressing the highest respect for law. p. 8 (III. A. 5.)

Of course, there is nothing new about this kind of civil disobedience. It was seen sublimely in the refusal of Shadrach, Meshach and Abednego to obey the laws of Nebuchadnezzar, because a higher moral law was involved. It was practiced superbly by the early Christians, who were willing to face hungry lions and the excruciating pain of chopping blocks before submitting to certain unjust laws of the Roman Empire. To a degree, academic freedom is a reality today because Socrates practiced civil disobedience. p. 8 (III. B.)

Extremism

You spoke of our activity in Birmingham as extreme. At first I was rather disappointed that fellow clergymen would see my nonviolent efforts as those of the extremist. I started thinking about the fact that I stand in the middle of two opposing forces in the Negro community. One is a force of complacency made up of Negroes who, as a result of long years of oppression, have been so completely drained of self-respect and a sense of "somebodiness" that they have adjusted to segregation, and of a few Negroes in the middle class who, because of a degree of academic and economic security, and because at points they profit by segregation, have unconsciously become insensitive to the problems of the masses. The other force is one of bitterness and hatred and comes perilously close to advocating violence. It is expressed in the various black nationalist groups that are springing up over the nation, the largest and best known being Elijah Muhammad's Muslim movement. This movement is nourished by the contemporary frustration over the continued existence of racial discrimination. It is made up of people who have lost faith in America, who have absolutely repudiated Christianity, and who have concluded that the white man is an incurable" devil." p. 11 (III. G. 1.)

But as I continued to think about the matter I gradually gained a bit of satisfaction from being considered an extremist. Was not Jesus an extremist in love? "Love your enemies, bless them that curse you, pray for them that despitefully use you." Was not Amos an extremist for justice -- "Let justice roll down like waters and righteousness like a mighty stream." Was not Paul an extremist for the gospel of Jesus Christ-- "I bear in my body the marks of the Lord Jesus." Was not Martin Luther an extremist -- "Here I stand; I can do none other so help me God." Was not John Bunyan an extremist -- "I will stay in jail to the end of my days before I make a butchery of my conscience." Was not Abraham Lincoln an extremist -- "This nation cannot survive half slave and half free." Was not Thomas Jefferson an extremist -- "We hold these truths to be self-evident, that all men are created equal." p. 12 (IV. B.)

So the question is not whether we will be extremist but what kind of extremist will we be. Will we be extremists for hate or will we be extremists for love? Will we be extremists for the preservation of injustice -- or will we be extremists for the cause of justice? In that dramatic scene on Calvary's hill three men were crucified. We must never forget that all three were crucified for the same crime -- the crime of extremism. Two were extremists for immorality, and thus fell below their environment. The other, Jesus Christ, was an extremist for love, truth, and goodness and thereby rose above His environment So, after all, maybe the South, the nation, and the world are in dire need of creative extremists p. 12 (IV. B.)

Injustice
Beyond this, I am in Birmingham because injustice is here. Just as the eighth century prophets left their little villages and carried their "thus saith the Lord" far beyond the boundaries of their home town, and just as the Apostle Paul left his little village of Tarsus and carried the gospel of Jesus Christ to practically every hamlet and city of the Graeco-Roman world, I too am compelled to carry the gospel of freedom beyond my particular home town. Like Paul, I must constantly respond to the Macedonian call for aid. p. 1 (II. A. 2.)

Injustice anywhere is a threat to justice everywhere. We are caught in an inescapable network of mutuality, tied in a single garment of destiny. Whatever affects one directly, affects all indirectly. Never again can we afford to live with the narrow, provincial "outside agitator" idea. Anyone who lives inside the United States can never be considered an outsider anywhere in this country. p. 2 (II. A. 3.)

Like a boil that can never be cured so long as it is covered up but must be opened with all its pus-flowing ugliness to the natural medicines of air and light, injustice must be exposed, with all the tension its exposure creates, to the light of human conscience and the air of national opinion before it can be cured. p. 9 (III. D. 2.)

Just & Unjust Laws
One may now ask: "How can you advocate breaking some laws and obeying others?" The answer lies in the fact that there are two types of laws: just and unjust. I would be the first to advocate obeying just laws. One has not only a legal but a moral responsibility to obey just laws. Conversely, one has a moral responsibility to disobey unjust laws. I would agree with St. Augustine that "an unjust law is no law at all." p. 6 (II. F. 2.)

Now, what is the difference between the two? How does one determine whether a law is just or unjust? A just law is a man-made code that squares with the moral law or the law of God. An unjust law is a code that is out of harmony with the moral law. To put it in the terms of St. Thomas Aquinas: An unjust law is a human law that is not rooted in eternal law and natural law. Any law that uplifts human personality is just. Any law that degrades human personality is unjust. All segregation statutes are unjust because segregation distorts the soul and damages the personality. It gives the segregator a false sense of superiority and the segregated a false sense of inferiority. pp. 6-7 (III. A. 1.)

An unjust law is a code that a majority inflicts on a minority that is not binding on itself. This is difference made legal. By the same token, a just law is a code that a majority compels a minority to follow and that it is willing to follow itself. This is sameness made legal. p. 7. (III. A. 2.)

An unjust law is a code inflicted upon a minority which that minority had not part in enacting or creating because they did not have an unhampered right to vote. p. 7 (III. A. 3.)

There are some instances when a law is just on its face but unjust in its application. p. 7. (III. A. 4.)

We should never forget that everything Adolf Hitler did in Germany was "legal" and everything the Hungarian freedom fighters did in Hungary was "illegal." It was "illegal" to aid and comfort a Jew in Hitler's Germany. p. 8 (III. C.)

Justice Delayed

For years now I have heard the word "Wait!" It rings in the ear of every Negro with piercing familiarity. This "Wait" has almost always meant 'Never.' We must come to see, with one of our distinguished jurists, that "justice too long delayed is justice denied." p. 5 (II. E.)

We have waited for more than 340 years for our constitutional and God-given rights. The nations of Asia and Africa are moving with jet-like speed toward gaining political independence, but we still creep at horse-and-buggy pace toward gaining a cup of coffee at a lunch counter. I guess it is easy for those who have never felt the stinging dark of segregation to say, "Wait." . . . when you are harried by day and haunted by night by the fact that you are a Negro, living constantly at tiptoe stance, never quite knowing what to expect next, and are plagued with inner fears and outer resentments; when you are forever fighting a degenerating sense of "nobodiness" then you will understand why we find it difficult to wait. There comes a time when the cup of endurance runs over, and men are no longer willing to be plunged into an abyss of injustice where they experience the bleakness or corroding despair. I hope, sirs, you can understand our legitimate and unavoidable impatience. p. 5-6 (II. F. 1.)

Law & Order

I must confess that over the past few years I have been gravely disappointed with the white moderate. I have almost reached the regrettable conclusion that the Negro's great stumbling block in his stride toward freedom is not the White Citizen's Counciler or the Ku Klux Klanner, but the white moderate, who is more devoted to "order" than to justice; who prefers a negative peace which is the absence of tension to a positive peace which is the presence of justice. p. 8-9 (III. D. 1.)

I had hoped that the white moderate would understand that law and order exist for the purpose of establishing justice and that when they fail in this purpose they become the dangerously structured dams that block the flow of social progress. p. 9 (III. D. 2.)

Over the past few years I have consistently preached that nonviolence demands that the means we use must be as pure as the ends we seek. I have tried to make clear that it is wrong to use immoral means to attain moral ends. But now I must affirm that it is just as wrong, or perhaps even more so, to use moral means to preserve immoral ends. Maybe Mr. Connor and his policemen have been rather publicly nonviolent, ... but they have used the moral means of nonviolence to maintain the immoral end of flagrant injustice. As T. S. Eliot has said that there is no greater treason than to do the right deed for the wrong reason. p. 18 (VII. A. 2.)

Non-Violence
In any nonviolent campaign there are four basic steps:
1. collection of the facts to determine whether injustices exist;
2. negotiation;
3. self-purification;
4. and direct action. p. 2 (II. B.)

We were not unmindful of the difficulties involved. So we decided to go through the process of self-purification. We started having workshops on nonviolence and repeatedly asked ourselves the questions,: "Are you able to accept blows without retaliating?" "Are you able to endure the ordeal of jail?" p. 3. (II. B. Step3.)

But I must confess that I am not afraid of the word tension. I have earnestly opposed violent tension, but there is a type of constructive, nonviolent tension which is necessary for growth. Just as Socrates felt that it was necessary to create a tension in the mind so that individuals could rise from the bondage of myths and half-truths to the unfettered realm of creative analysis and objective appraisal, we must we see the need for nonviolent gadflies to create the kind of tension in society that will help men rise from the dark depths of prejudice and racism to the majestic heights of understanding and brotherhood. p. 4 (II. C. 1.)

My friends, I must say to you that we have not made a single gain in civil rights without determined legal and nonviolent pressure. History is the long and tragic story of the fact that privileged groups seldom give up their privileges voluntarily. Individuals may see the moral light and voluntarily give up their unjust posture; but, as Reinhold Niebuhr has reminded us, groups tend to be more immoral than individuals. p. 4-5 (II. D.)

I have tried to stand between these two forces, saying that we need emulate neither the "do-nothingism" of the complacent nor the hatred and despair of the black nationalist. For there is the more excellent way of love and nonviolent protest. I am grateful to God that, through the Negro church, the dimension of nonviolence entered our struggle. Pp. 11 (III. G. 2.)

A TOPICAL INDEX OF BIBLICAL, THEOLOGICAL, PHILOSOPHICAL AND HISTORICAL REFERENCES IN

DR. MARTIN LUTHER KING JR.'S LETTER FROM BIRMINGHAM JAIL

AND TO THE EXPLANATORY NOTES

The "N." in the index citations below stands for "Note" referring to the endnotes. The numbers following the "N." refer to specific numbers of the endnotes. The bold font in the following index indicates that Dr. King actually used the referenced item in his *Letter* in the paragraph where the endnote number appears. The regular font indicates that the item is found in the annotations and was not directly written by Dr. King in his *Letter*.

Concepts of Martin Luther King's Non-Violence

"A Call For Unity"- N. 1, 5, 10
Albany Campaign - N. 127
Stride toward Freedom - N. 23, 24, 104
Birmingham Campaign - N. 28, 30, 127
Bus Boycott - N. 104
Civil Rights - N. 16, 28, 35, 37, 40, 98, 120, 152
Civil Disobedience - N. 46, 48, 49
Courage - N. 24, 104
Direct Action - N. 26, 34
Eliminating Evil - N. 24
Freedom Rides - N. 82
"I Have A Dream" - N. 105, 136, 154
Nonconformist - N. 114
Nonviolence - N. 23, 24, 25, 34, 46, 79, 104, 140
Persecution - N. 115
Reconciliation - N. 1, 11, 24, 38, 152, 154
Segregation - N. 11, 37, 39, 41, 44, 46, 96, 97, 98, 99, 100, 104
Self-Purification - N. 25
Sit-in - N. 26, 32, 145
Suffering - N. 24, 115, 123
Unjust Law - N. 42, 43.

People In Civil Rights Conflict

Ali, Muhammad - N.75
Abernathy, Ralph - N. 104
Barnett, Ross Robert - N. 110, 143
Birmingham Police - N. 138
Black Muslims - N. 75
Boutwell, Albert - N. 30, 35
Boyle, Sarah Patton - N. 95, 100
Braden, Ann - N. 95, 99
Carpenter, CCJ - N. 1, 4, 28
Chambliss, "Dynamite Bob" - N. 27
Clergymen - N. 1, 10, 11, 12, 152
Connor, Bull - N.30, 31,138
Cowan, Wayne H. - N. 36
Dabbs, James McBride - N. 95, 97
"Disturbers of the Peace" - N. 116
Durick, Joseph A. - N. 1, 3
Golden, Harry - N. 95, 97
Grafman, Rabbi Hilton L. - N. 1, 4
Gandhi, Mahatma - N. 23
Hardin, Bishop Paul - N. 1, 5
Harmon, Bishop Nolan B. - N. 1, 6
Ku Klux Klan - N. 2, 14, 27, 56, 57, 95, 138
Lincoln, C. Eric - N. 75
Malcolm X - N. 75
McGill, Ralph - N. 94, 95
McWhorter, Diane- N. 27

DR. MARTIN LUTHER KING JR.'S LETTER FROM BIRMINGHAM JAIL

WITH ENDNOTES SHOWING HIS EDITS FOR THE FINAL VERSION

APRIL 16, 1963

My dear Fellow Clergymen,

While confined here in the Birmingham City Jail, I came across your recent statement calling our present activities "unwise and untimely." Seldom, if ever, do I pause to answer criticism of my work and ideas. If I sought to answer all the criticisms that cross my desk, my secretaries would be engaged in little else in the course of the day and I would have no time for constructive work. But since I feel that you are men of genuine goodwill and your criticisms are sincerely set forth, I would like to answer your statement in what I hope will be patient and reasonable terms.

I think I should give the reason for my being in Birmingham, since you have been influenced by the argument of "outsiders coming in." I have the honor of serving as president of the Southern Christian Leadership Conference, an organization operating in every Southern state with headquarters in Atlanta, Georgia. We have some eighty-five affiliate organizations all across the South -- one being the Alabama Christian Movement for Human Rights. Whenever necessary and possible we share staff, educational, and financial resources with our affiliates. Several months ago our local affiliate here in Birmingham invited us to be on call to engage in a nonviolent direct action program if such were deemed necessary. We readily consented and when the hour came we lived up to our promises. So I am here, along with several members of my staff, because we were invited here. I am here because I have basic organizational ties here. Beyond this, I am in Birmingham because injustice is here. Just as the eighth century[1] prophets left their little villages and carried their "thus saith the Lord" far beyond the boundaries of their home town, and just as the Apostle Paul left his little village of Tarsus and carried the gospel of Jesus Christ to practically every hamlet and city of the Graeco-Roman world, I too am compelled to carry the gospel of freedom beyond my particular home town. Like Paul, I must constantly respond to the Macedonian call for aid.

Moreover, I am cognizant of the interrelatedness of all communities and states. I cannot sit idly by in Atlanta and not be concerned about what happens in Birmingham. Injustice anywhere is a threat to justice everywhere. We are caught in an inescapable network of mutuality tied in a single garment of destiny. Whatever affects one directly affects all indirectly. Never again can we afford to live with the narrow, provincial "outside agitator" idea. Anyone who lives inside the United States can never be considered an outsider anywhere in this country.[2]

You deplore the demonstrations that are presently taking place in Birmingham. But I am sorry that your statement did not express a similar concern for the conditions that brought the demonstrations into being. I am sure that each of you would want to go beyond the superficial social analyst who looks merely at effects, and does not grapple with underlying causes. I would not hesitate to say that it is unfortunate that so-called demonstrations are taking place in Birmingham at this time, but I would say in more emphatic terms that it is even more unfortunate that the white power structure of this city left the Negro community with no other alternative.

In any nonviolent campaign there are four basic steps:
(1) Collection of the facts to determine whether injustices
are alive; (2) Negotiation; (3) Self-purification; and (4)
Direct action. We have gone through all of these steps in
Birmingham. There can be no gainsaying of the fact that
racial injustice engulfs this community. Birmingham
is probably the most thoroughly segregated city in the
United States. Its ugly record of police brutality is known
in every section of this country. Its unjust treatment of
Negroes in the courts is a notorious reality. There have
been more unsolved bombings of Negro homes and churches
in Birmingham than any city in this nation. These are the
hard, brutal, and unbelievable facts. On the basis of these
conditions Negro leaders sought to negotiate with the city
fathers. But the political leaders consistently refused to
engage in good faith negotiation.

Then came the opportunity last September to talk
with some of the leaders of the economic community. In
these negotiating sessions certain promises were made
by the merchants -- such as the promise to remove the
humiliating racial signs from the stores. On the basis of
these promises Rev. Shuttlesworth and the leaders of the
Alabama Christian Movement for Human Rights agreed to
call a moratorium on any type of demonstrations. As the
weeks and months unfolded we realized that we were the
victims of a broken promise. The signs remained.[3] As in
so many experiences of the past we were confronted with
blasted hopes, and the dark shadow of a deep disappointment
settled upon us. So we had no alternative except that of
preparing for direct action, whereby we would present
our very bodies as a means of laying our case before the
conscience of the local and national community. We were
not unmindful of the difficulties involved. So we decided
to go through a process of self-purification. We started
having workshops on nonviolence and repeatedly asked
ourselves the questions, "Are you able to accept blows

without retaliating?" "Are you able to endure the ordeals of jail?"

We decided to set our direct-action program around the Easter season, realizing that with the exception of Christmas, this was the largest shopping period of the year. Knowing that a strong economic withdrawal program would be the by-product of direct action, we felt that this was the best time to bring pressure on the merchants for the needed changes. Then it occurred to us that the March[4] election was ahead, and so we speedily decided to postpone action until after election day. When we discovered that Mr. Connor[5] was in the run-off[6], we decided again to postpone action[7] so that the demonstrations could not be used to cloud the issues. At this time we agreed to begin our nonviolent witness the day after the run-off.

This reveals that we did not move irresponsibly into direct action.[8] We too wanted to see Mr. Connor defeated; so we went through postponement after postponement to aid in this community need. After this we felt that direct action could be delayed no longer.

You may well ask, Why direct action? Why sit-ins, marches, etc.? Isn't negotiation a better path?" You are exactly right in your call for negotiation. Indeed, this is the purpose of direct action. Nonviolent direct action seeks to create such a crisis and establish such creative tension that a community that has constantly refused to negotiate is forced to confront the issue. It seeks so to dramatize the issue that it can no longer be ignored. I just referred to the creation of tension as a part of the work of the nonviolent resister. This may sound rather shocking. But I must confess that I am not afraid of the word tension. I have earnestly worked and preached against violent tension, but there is a type of constructive nonviolent tension that is necessary for growth. Just as Socrates felt that it was necessary to create a tension in the mind so that individuals could rise from the bondage of myths and half-truths to the unfettered realm of creative analysis and objective appraisal, we must see the need of having nonviolent gadflies to create the kind of tension in society that will help men rise from the dark depths of prejudice and racism to the majestic heights of understanding and brotherhood. So the purpose of the[9] direct action is to create a situation so crisis-packed that it will inevitably open the door to negotiation. We,[10] therefore, concur with you in your call for negotiation. Too long has our beloved Southland been bogged down in the tragic attempt to live in monologue rather than dialogue.

One of the basic points in your statement is that our acts are[11] untimely. Some have asked, "Why didn't you give the new administration time to act?" The only answer that I can give to this inquiry is that the new administration must be prodded about as much as the outgoing one before it acts. We will be sadly mistaken if we feel that the election of Mr. Boutwell will bring the millennium to Birmingham. While Mr. Boutwell is much more articulate and gentle than Mr. Connor, they are both segregationists dedicated to the task of maintaining the status quo. The hope I see in Mr. Boutwell is that he will be reasonable enough to see the futility of massive resistance to desegregation. But he will not see this without pressure from the devotees of civil rights. My friends, I must say to you that we have not made a single gain in civil rights without determined legal and nonviolent pressure. History is the long and tragic story of the fact[12] that privileged groups seldom give up their privileges voluntarily. Individuals may see the moral light and voluntarily give up their unjust posture; but as Reinhold Niebuhr has reminded us, groups are more immoral than individuals.

We know through painful experience that freedom

is never voluntarily given by the oppressor; it must be demanded by the oppressed. Frankly I have never yet engaged in a direct action movement that was "well timed," according to the timetable of those who have not suffered unduly from the disease of segregation. For years now I have heard the word "Wait!" It rings in the ear of every Negro with a piercing familiarity. This "wait" has almost always meant "never." It has been a tranquilizing thalidomide, relieving the emotional stress for a moment, only to give birth to an ill-formed infant of frustration.[13] We must come to see with the distinguished jurist of yesterday that "justice too long delayed is justice denied." We have waited for more than three hundred and forty years for our constitutional and God-given rights. The nations of Asia and Africa are moving with jet-like speed toward the goal of political independence, and we still creep at horse and buggy pace toward the gaining of a cup of coffee at a lunch counter.

I guess it is easy for those who have never felt the stinging darts of segregation to say wait. But when you have seen vicious mobs lynch your mothers and fathers at will and drown your sisters and brothers at whim; when you have seen hate filled policemen curse, kick, brutalize,[14] and even kill your black brothers and sisters with impunity;[15] when you see the vast majority of your twenty million Negro brothers smothering in an air-tight cage of poverty in the midst of an affluent society; when you suddenly find your tongue twisted and your speech stammering as you seek to explain to your six-year-old daughter why she can't go to the public amusement park that has just been advertised on television, and see tears welling up in her little eyes when she is told that Funtown is closed to colored children, and see the depressing[16] clouds of inferiority begin to form in her little mental sky, and see her begin to distort her little personality by unconsciously developing a bitterness toward white people; when you have to concoct an answer for a five-year-old son asking in agonizing pathos: "Daddy, why do white people treat colored people so mean?"; when you take a cross-country drive and find it necessary to sleep night after night in the uncomfortable corners of your automobile because no motel will accept you; when you are humiliated day in and day out by nagging signs reading "white" men and "colored"; when your first name becomes "nigger" and your middle name becomes "boy" (however old you are) and your last name becomes "John," and when your wife and mother are never given the respected title "Mrs."; when you are harried by day and haunted by night by the fact that you are a Negro, living constantly at tip-toe stance never quite knowing what to expect next, and plagued with inner fears and outer resentments; when you are forever fighting a degenerating sense of "nobodiness" -- then you will understand why we find it difficult to wait. There comes a time when the cup of endurance runs over, and men are no longer willing to be plunged into an abyss of injustice where they experience the bleakness of corroding[17] despair. I hope, sirs, you can understand our legitimate and unavoidable impatience.

You express a great deal of anxiety over our willingness to break laws. This is certainly a legitimate concern. Since we so diligently urge people to obey the Supreme Court's decision of 1954 outlawing segregation in the public schools,[18] it is rather strange and paradoxical to find us consciously breaking laws. One may well ask: "How can you advocate breaking some laws and obeying others?" The answer is found in the fact that there are two types of laws: There are just laws and there are unjust laws. I would be the first to advocate obeying just laws. One has not only a legal but moral responsibility to obey just laws. Conversely, one has a moral responsibility to disobey unjust laws. I would agree with Saint Augustine that "An unjust law is no law at all."

Now what is the difference between the two? How does one determine when a law is just or unjust? A just law is a man-made code that squares with the moral law or the law of God. An unjust law is a code that is out of harmony with the moral law. To put it in the terms of Saint Thomas Aquinas, an unjust law is a human law that is not rooted in eternal and natural law. Any law that uplifts human personality is just. Any law that degrades human personality is unjust. All segregation statutes are unjust because segregation distorts the soul and damages the personality. It gives the segregator a false sense of superiority and the segregated a false sense of inferiority. To use the words of Martin Buber, the great Jewish philosopher, segregation substitutes an "I-it" relationship for an "I-thou" relationship, and ends up relegating persons to the status of things. So segregation is not only politically, economically, and sociologically unsound, but it is morally wrong and sinful.[19] Paul Tillich has said that sin is separation. Isn't segregation an existential expression of man's tragic separation, an expression of his awful estrangement, his terrible sinfulness? So I can urge men to obey the 1954 decision of the Supreme Court because it is morally right, and I can urge them to disobey segregation ordinances because they are morally wrong.

Let us turn to a more concrete example of just and unjust laws. An unjust law is a code that a[20] majority inflicts on a minority that is not binding on itself. This is difference made legal. On the other hand a just law is a code that a majority compels a minority to follow that it is willing to follow itself. This is sameness made legal.

Let me give another explanation. An unjust law is a code inflicted upon a minority which that minority had no part in enacting or creating because they did not have the unhampered right to vote. Who can say that the legislature of Alabama which set up the segregation laws was democratically elected? Throughout the state of Alabama all types of conniving[21] methods are used to prevent Negroes from becoming registered voters and there are some counties without a single Negro registered to vote despite the fact that the Negro constitutes a majority of the population. Can any law set up in such a state be considered democratically structured?

These are just a few examples of unjust and just laws.[22] There are some instances when a law is just on its face but unjust in its application. For instance, I was arrested Friday[23] on a charge of parading without a permit. Now there is nothing wrong with an ordinance which requires a permit for a parade, but when the ordinance is used to preserve segregation and to deny citizens the First Amendment privilege of peaceful assembly and peaceful protest, then it becomes unjust.

I hope you can see the distinction I am trying to point out. In no sense do I advocate evading or defying the law as the rabid segregationist would do. This would lead to anarchy. One who breaks an unjust law must do it openly, lovingly (not hatefully as the white mothers did in New Orleans when they were seen on television screaming "nigger, nigger, nigger")[24] and with a willingness to accept the penalty. I submit that an individual who breaks a law that conscience tells him is unjust, and willingly accepts the penalty by staying in jail[25] to arouse the conscience of the community over its injustice, is in reality expressing the very highest respect for law.

Of course there is nothing new about this kind of civil disobedience. It was seen sublimely in the refusal of Shadrach, Meshach, and Abednego to obey the laws of Nebuchadnezzar because a higher moral law was involved. It was practiced superbly by the early Christians who were willing to face hungry lions and the excruciating pain of chopping blocks, before submitting to certain unjust laws of the Roman Empire. To a degree academic freedom is a reality today because Socrates practiced civil disobedience.[26]

We can never forget that everything Hitler did in Germany was "legal" and everything the Hungarian freedom fighters did in Hungary was "illegal." It was "illegal" to aid and comfort a Jew in Hitler's Germany. But I am sure that, if I had lived in Germany during that time, I would have aided and comforted my Jewish brothers even though it was illegal.[27] If I lived in a communist country today where certain principles dear to the Christian faith are suppressed, I believe I would openly advocate disobeying these anti-religious laws.

I must make two honest confessions to you, my Christian and Jewish brothers. First, I must confess that over the last few years I have been gravely disappointed with the white moderate. I have almost reached the regrettable conclusion that the Negroes' great stumbling block in the stride toward freedom is not the White Citizen's "Counciler" or the Ku Klux Klanner, but the white moderate who is more devoted to "order" than to justice; who prefers a negative peace which is the absence of tension to a positive peace which is the presence of justice; who constantly says "I agree with you in the goal you seek, but I can't agree with your methods of direct action"; who paternalistically feels that he can set the timetable for another man's freedom; who lives by the myth of time[28] and who constantly advises the Negro to wait until a "more convenient season." Shallow understanding from people of good will is more frustrating than absolute misunderstanding from people of ill will. Lukewarm acceptance is much more bewildering than outright rejection.

I had hoped that the white moderate would understand

that law and order exist for the purpose of establishing justice, and that when they fail to do this they become dangerously structured dams that block the flow of social progress. I had hoped that the white moderate would understand that the present tension in the South is merely a necessary phase of the transition from an obnoxious negative peace, where the Negro passively accepted his unjust plight, to a substance-filled positive peace, where all men will respect the dignity and worth of human personality. Actually, we who engage in nonviolent direct action are not the creators of tension. We merely bring to the surface the hidden tension that is already alive. We bring it out in the open where it can be seen and dealt with. Like a boil that can never be cured as long as it is covered up but must be opened with all its pus-flowing[29] ugliness to the natural medicines of air and light, injustice must likewise be exposed, with all of the tension its exposing creates, to the light of human conscience and the air of national opinion before it can be cured.

In your statement you asserted that our actions, even though peaceful, must be condemned because they precipitate violence. But can this assertion be logically made? Isn't this like condemning the robbed man because his possession of money precipitated the evil act of robbery? Isn't this like condemning Socrates because his unswerving commitment to truth and his philosophical delvings[30] precipitated the misguided popular mind to make him drink the hemlock? Isn't this like condemning Jesus because His unique God consciousness and never-ceasing devotion to His[31] will precipitated the evil act of crucifixion? We must come to see, as federal courts have consistently affirmed, that it is immoral[32] to urge an individual to withdraw[33] his efforts to gain his basic constitutional rights because the quest precipitates violence. Society must protect the robbed and punish the robber.

I had also hoped that the white moderate would reject the myth of time.[34] I received a letter this morning from a white brother in Texas which said: "All Christians know that the colored people will receive equal rights eventually, but is it possible that you are in too great of a religious hurry?[35] It has taken Christianity almost 2,000 years to accomplish what it has. The teachings of Christ take time to come to earth." All that is said here grows out of a tragic misconception of time. It is the strangely irrational notion[36] that there is something in the very flow of time that will inevitably cure all ills. Actually time is neutral. It can be used either destructively or constructively. I am coming to feel that the people of ill will have used time much more effectively than the people of good will. We will have to repent in this generation not merely for the vitriolic[37] words and actions of the bad people, but for the appalling silence of the good people. We must come to see that human progress never rolls in on wheels of inevitability. It comes through the tireless efforts and persistent work[38] of men willing to be co-workers with God, and without this hard work time itself becomes an ally of the forces of social stagnation.

We must use time creatively, and forever realize[39] that the time is always ripe to do right. Now is the time to make real the promise of democracy, and transform our pending national elegy into a creative psalm of brotherhood. Now is the time to lift our national policy from the quicksand of racial injustice to the solid rock of human dignity.

You spoke of our activity in Birmingham as extreme. At first I was rather disappointed that fellow clergymen would see my nonviolent efforts as those of the extremist. I started thinking about the fact that I stand in the middle of two opposing forces in the Negro community. One is a force of complacency made up of Negroes who, as a result of long years of oppression, have been so completely drained of self-respect and a sense of "somebodiness" that they have adjusted to segregation, and of a few Negroes in the middle class who, because of a degree of academic and economic security, and because at points they profit by segregation, have unconsciously become insensitive to the problems of the masses. The other force is one of bitterness and hatred and comes perilously close to advocating violence. It is expressed in the various black nationalist groups that are springing up over the nation, the largest and best known being Elijah Muhammad's Muslim movement. This movement is nourished by the contemporary frustration[40] over the continued existence of racial discrimination. It is made up of people who have lost faith in America, who have absolutely repudiated Christianity, and who have concluded that the white man is an incurable[41] "devil." I have tried to stand between these two forces saying that we need not follow the "do-nothingism" of the complacent or the hatred and despair of the black nationalist. There is the more excellent way of love and nonviolent protest. I'm grateful to God that, through the Negro church, the dimension of nonviolence entered[42] our struggle. If this philosophy had not emerged I am convinced that by now many streets of the South would be flowing with floods of blood. And I am further convinced that if our white brothers dismiss us as "rabble rousers" and "outside agitators" -- those of us who are working through the channels of nonviolent direct action -- and refuse to support our nonviolent efforts, millions of Negroes, out of frustration and despair, will seek solace and security in black-nationalist ideologies, a development that will lead inevitably to a frightening racial nightmare.

Oppressed people cannot remain oppressed forever. The urge for freedom will eventually come. This is what has happened to the American Negro. Something within has reminded him of his birthright of freedom; something without has reminded him that he can gain it. Consciously and unconsciously, he has been swept in by what the Germans call the Zeitgeist, and with his black brothers of Africa, and his brown and yellow brothers of Asia, South America, and the Caribbean, he is moving with a sense of cosmic[43] urgency toward the promised land of racial justice. Recognizing this vital urge that has engulfed the Negro community, one should readily understand public demonstrations. The Negro has many pent-up resentments and latent frustrations. He has to get them out. So let him march sometime; let him have his prayer pilgrimages to the city hall; understand why he must have sit-ins[44] and freedom rides. If his repressed emotions do not come out in these nonviolent ways, they will come out in ominous expressions[45] of violence. This is not a threat; it is a fact of history. So I have not said to my people, "Get rid of your discontent." But I have tried to say that this normal and healthy discontent can be channeled through the creative outlet of nonviolent direct action. Now this approach is being dismissed as extremist. I must admit that I was initially disappointed in being so categorized.[46]

But as I continued to think about the matter I gradually gained a bit of satisfaction from being considered an extremist. Was not Jesus an extremist in love? "Love your enemies, bless them that curse you, pray for them that despitefully use you."[47] Was not Amos an extremist for justice -- "Let justice roll down like waters and righteousness like a mighty stream." Was not Paul an extremist for the gospel of Jesus Christ[48] -- "I bear in my body the marks of the Lord Jesus." Was not Martin Luther an extremist -- "Here I stand; I can do none other so help me God." Was not John Bunyan an extremist[49] -- "I will stay in jail to the end of my days before I make a butchery of my conscience." Was not Abraham Lincoln an extremist -- "This nation cannot survive half slave and half free." Was not Thomas Jefferson an extremist -- "We hold these truths to be self-evident, that all men are created equal." So the question is not whether we will be extremist but what kind of extremist will we be. Will we be extremists for hate or will we be extremists for love? Will we be extremists for the preservation of injustice -- or will we be extremists for the cause of justice? In that dramatic scene on Calvary's hill three men were crucified. We must never forget that all three were crucified for the same crime -- the crime of extremism. Two were extremists for immorality, and thus fell below their environment. The other, Jesus Christ, was an extremist for love, truth, and goodness, and thereby rose above His environment. So, after all, maybe the South, the nation, and the world are in dire need of creative extremists.

I had hoped that the white moderate would see this.[50] Maybe I was too optimistic. Maybe I expected too much. I guess I should have realized that few members of a race that has oppressed another race can understand or appreciate[51] the deep groans and passionate yearnings of those that have been oppressed, and still fewer have the vision to see that injustice must be rooted out by strong, persistent, and determined action. I am thankful, however, that some of our white brothers have grasped the meaning of this social revolution and committed themselves to it. They are still all too small in quantity, but they are big in quality. Some like Ralph McGill, Lillian Smith, Harry Golden, and James Dabbs[52] have written about our struggle in eloquent, prophetic, and understanding[53] terms. Others have marched with us down nameless streets of the South. They have languished in filthy, roach-infested jails, suffering the abuse and brutality of angry[54] policemen who see them as "dirty nigger lovers." They, unlike so many of their moderate brothers and sisters, have recognized the urgency of the moment and sensed the need for powerful "action" antidotes to combat the disease of segregation.

Let me rush on to mention[55] my other[56] disappointment.

I have been so greatly disappointed with the white Church and its leadership. Of course there are some notable exceptions. I am not unmindful of the fact that each of you has taken some significant stands on this issue. I commend you, Rev. Stallings, for your Christian stand on this past Sunday, in welcoming Negroes to your worship service on a non-segregated basis. I commend the Catholic leaders of this state for integrating Spring Hill College several years ago.

But despite these notable exceptions I must honestly reiterate that I have been disappointed with the Church. I do not say that as one of those negative critics who can always find something wrong with the Church. I say it as a minister of the gospel, who loves the Church; who was nurtured in its bosom; who has been sustained by its spiritual blessings and who will remain true to it as long as the cord of life shall lengthen.

I had the strange feeling[57] when I was suddenly catapulted into the leadership of the bus protest in Montgomery[58] several years ago that we would have the support of the white Church. I felt that the white ministers, priests, and rabbis of the South would be some of our strongest allies. Instead, some have been outright opponents, refusing to understand the freedom movement and misrepresenting its leaders; all too many others have been more cautious than courageous and have remained silent behind the anesthetizing security of the stained glass windows.

In spite of my shattered dreams of the past,[59] I came to Birmingham with the hope that the white religious leadership of this community would see the justice of our cause and with deep moral concern, serve as the channel through which our just grievances could get to the power structure. I had hoped that each of you would understand. But again I have been disappointed.

I have heard numerous religious leaders of the South call upon their worshippers to comply with a desegregation decision because it is the law, but I have longed to hear white ministers say follow this decree because integration is morally right and the Negro is your brother. In the midst of blatant injustices inflicted upon the Negro, I have watched white churches[60] stand on the sideline and merely mouth pious irrelevancies and sanctimonious trivialities. In the midst of a mighty struggle to rid our nation of racial and economic injustice, I have heard so many ministers say, "Those are social issues with which the gospel has no real concern," and I have watched so many churches commit themselves to a completely other-worldly religion which made[61] a strange[62] distinction between body and soul, the sacred and the secular.

So here we are moving toward the exit of the twentieth century with a religious community largely adjusted to the status quo, standing as a tail-light behind other community agencies rather than a headlight leading men to higher levels of justice.[63]

I have travelled the length and breadth of Alabama, Mississippi and all the other southern states. On sweltering summer days and crisp autumn mornings I have looked at her beautiful churches with their[64] spires pointing heavenward. I have beheld the impressive outlay[65] of her massive religious education buildings. Over and over again I have found myself asking: "Who worships here?[66] Who is their God? Where were their voices when the lips of Governor Barnett dripped with words of interposition and nullification? Where were they when Governor Wallace gave the clarion call for defiance and hatred? Where were their voices of support when tired,[67] bruised, and weary Negro men and women decided to rise from the dark dungeons of complacency to the bright hills of creative protest?"

Yes, these questions are still in my mind. In deep disappointment, I have wept over the laxity of the church. But be assured that my tears have been tears of love. There can be no deep disappointment where there is not deep love. Yes, I love the Church; I love her sacred walls.[68] How could I do otherwise? I am in the rather unique position of being the son, the grandson, and the great-grandson of preachers. Yes, I see the Church as the body of Christ. But, oh! How we have blemished and scarred that body through social neglect and fear of being nonconformist.[69]

There was a time when the Church was very powerful. It was during that period when the early Christians rejoiced when they were deemed worthy to suffer for what they believed. In those days the Church was not merely a thermometer that recorded the ideas and principles of popular opinion; it was a thermostat that transformed the mores of society. Wherever the early Christians entered a town the power structure got disturbed and immediately sought to convict them for being "disturbers of the peace" and "outside agitators." But they[70] went on with the conviction that they were "a colony of heaven" and had to obey God rather than man. They were small in number but big in commitment. They were too God-intoxicated to be "astronomically intimidated." They[71] brought an end to such ancient evils as infanticide and gladiatorial contest.72

Things are different now. The contemporary Church is so often a weak, ineffectual voice with an uncertain sound. It is so often the arch-supporter[73] of the status quo. Far from being disturbed by the presence of the Church, the power structure of the average community is consoled by the Church's silent and often[74] vocal sanction of things as they are.

But the judgment of God is upon the Church as never

before. If the Church of today does not recapture the sacrificial spirit of the early Church, it will lose its authentic ring,[75] forfeit the loyalty of millions, and be dismissed as an irrelevant social club with no meaning for the twentieth century. I am meeting young people every day whose disappointment with the Church has risen to outright disgust.

Maybe again I have been too optimistic. Is organized religion too inextricably bound to the status quo to save our nation and the world? Maybe I must turn my faith to the inner spiritual Church, the church within the Church, as the true ecclesia and the hope of the world. But again I am thankful to God that some noble souls from the ranks of organized religion have broken loose from the paralyzing chains of conformity and joined us as active partners in the struggle for freedom. They have left their secure congregations and walked the streets of Albany, Georgia, with us. They have gone through the highways of the South on torturous rides for freedom.[76] Yes, they have gone to jail with us.[77] Some have been kicked out of[78] their churches and lost the support of their bishops and fellow ministers. But they have gone with the faith that right defeated is stronger than evil triumphant. These men have been the leaven in the lump of the race.[79] Their witness has been the spiritual salt that has preserved the true meaning of the Gospel in these troubled times. They have carved a tunnel of hope through the dark mountain of disappointment.

I hope the Church as a whole will meet the challenge of this decisive hour. But even if the Church does not come to the aid of justice, I have no despair about the future. I have no fear about the outcome of our struggle in Birmingham, even if our motives are presently misunderstood. We will reach the goal of freedom in Birmingham and all over the nation, because the goal of America is freedom. Abused and scorned though we may be, our destiny is tied up with the destiny of America. Before the pilgrims landed at Plymouth, we were here. Before the pen of Jefferson etched across the pages of history the majestic words of the Declaration of Independence, we were here. For more than two centuries our foreparents[80] labored in this country without wages; they made cotton "king"; and they built the homes of their masters in the midst of brutal injustice[81] and shameful humiliation -- and yet out of a bottomless vitality they continued to thrive and develop. If the inexpressible cruelties of slavery could not stop us, the opposition we now face will surely fail. We will win our freedom because the sacred heritage of our nation and the eternal will of God are embodied in our echoing demands.

I must close now.[82] But before closing I am impelled to mention one other point in your statement that troubled me profoundly. You warmly commend the Birmingham police force for keeping "order" and "preventing violence." I don't believe you would have so warmly commended the police force if you had seen its angry violent dogs literally biting six unarmed, nonviolent Negroes.[83] I don't believe you would so quickly commend the policemen if you would observe their ugly and inhuman treatment of Negroes here in the city jail; if you would watch them push and curse old Negro women and young Negro girls; if you would see them slap and kick old Negro men and young Negro[84] boys; if you will observe them, as they did on two occasions, refuse to give us food because we wanted to sing our grace together. I'm sorry that[85] I can't join you in your praise for the police department.

It is true that they have been rather disciplined in their public handling of the demonstrators. In this sense they have been rather publicly "nonviolent." But for what purpose? To preserve the evil system of segregation. Over the last few years I have consistently preached that nonviolence demands the means we use must be as pure as the ends we seek. So I have tried to make it clear that it is wrong to use immoral means to attain moral ends. But now I must affirm that it is just as wrong or even more so to use moral means to preserve immoral ends. Maybe Mr. Connor and his policemen have been rather publicly nonviolent, as Chief Pritchett was in Albany, Georgia, but they have used the moral means of nonviolence to maintain the immoral end of flagrant[86] injustice. T. S. Eliot has said that there is no greater treason than to do the right deed for the wrong reason.[87]

I wish you had commended the Negro sit-inners and demonstrators of Birmingham for their sublime courage, their willingness to suffer, and their amazing discipline in the midst of the most inhuman provocation.[88] One day the South will recognize its real heroes. They will be the James Merediths, courageously and with a majestic[89] sense of purpose, facing jeering and hostile mobs and the agonizing loneliness that characterizes the life of the pioneer. They will be old, oppressed, battered Negro women, symbolized in a seventy-two year old woman of Montgomery, Alabama, who rose up with a sense of dignity and with her people decided not to ride the segregated buses, and responded to one who inquired about her tiredness with ungrammatical profundity: "My feets is tired, but my soul is rested." They will be the young high school and college students, young ministers of the gospel and a host of their elders courageously and nonviolently sitting-in at lunch counters and willingly going to jail for conscience sake. One day the South will know that when these disinherited children of God sat down at lunch counters they were in reality standing up for the best in the American dream and the most sacred values in our Judaeo-Christian heritage, and thus carrying our whole nation[90] back to great wells of democracy which were dug deep by the founding fathers in the formulation of the Constitution and the Declaration of Independence.

Never before have I written a letter this long (or should I say a book?).[91] I'm afraid it is much too long to take your precious time. I can assure you that it would have been much shorter if I had been writing from a comfortable desk, but what else is there to do when you are alone for days in the dull monotony[92] of a narrow jail cell other than write long letters, think strange[93] thoughts, and pray long prayers?

If I have said anything in this letter that is an overstatement of the truth and is indicative of an unreasonable impatience, I beg you to forgive me. If I have said anything in this letter that is an understatement of the truth and is indicative of my having a patience that makes me patient with[94] anything less than brotherhood, I beg God to forgive me.

I hope this letter finds you strong in the faith. I also hope that circumstances will soon make it possible for me to meet each of you, not as an integrationist or a civil rights leader, but as a fellow clergyman and a Christian brother. Let us all hope that the dark clouds of racial prejudice will soon pass away and the deep fog of misunderstanding will be lifted from our fear-drenched communities and in some not too distant tomorrow[95] the radiant stars of love and brotherhood will shine over our great nation with all their scintillating beauty.

Yours for the cause of
Peace and Brotherhood,

Martin Luther King, Jr.

LETTER ENDNOTES

1   In the final version, Dr. King adds here, "B.C.".

2   In the final version "in this country" is replaced by "anywhere within its bounds."

3   In the final version, Dr. King replaces "The signs remained" with "A few signs, briefly removed, returned; the others remained."

4   In the final version "March election" is replaced by "Birmingham's mayoralty election was coming up in March".

5   In the final version "Mr. Connor" is replaced with "the Commissioner of Police Safety, Eugene 'Bull' Connor".

6   In the final version "was in the run-off" is replaced by "had piled up enough votes to be in the run-off".

7   The final version adds "until the day after the run-off".

8   This sentence is deleted in the final version.

9   In the final version "the" is replaced by "our".

10   In the final version "we" is replaced by "I".

11   In the final version, "our acts are" is replaced with "the action that I and my associates have taken in Birmingham is".

12   In the final version, "History is the long and tragic story of the fact" is replaced by "Lamentably, it is an historical fact".

13   This entire sentence was deleted in the final version of the *Letter*.

14   Dr. King deletes the word "brutalize" in the final version of the *Letter*.

15   "With impunity" is deleted in the final version.

16   "Depressing" is replaced by "ominous" in the final version.

17   The words "an abyss of injustice where they experience the bleakness of corroding despair" are replaced in the final version by "the abyss of despair".

18   The final version adds "at first glance".

19   The word "sinful" is replaced by "awful" in the final version.

20   In the final version, "numerical or power" is added to modify "majority".

21   In the final version, "conniving" is replaced by "devious".

22   This sentence is deleted in the final version.

23   "Friday" is replaced by "I have been arrested" in the final version.

24   This parenthetical statement is deleted in the final version.

25   The final version replaces "accepts the penalty by staying in jail to arouse" with "accepts the penalty of imprisonment in order to arouse".

26   In the final version, Dr. King adds, "In our own nation, the Boston Tea Party represented a massive act of civil disobedience." For a discussion of the Boston Tea Party see note 52.

27   In the final version, Dr. King deletes, "even though it was illegal".

28   In the final version "the myth of time" is replaced by "a mythical concept of time".

29   In the final version, Dr. King deletes "pus-flowing".

30   In the final version "delvings" is replaced by "inquiries".

31   In the final version, "His" is replaced with "God".

32   In the final version, "immoral" is replaced with "wrong".

33   In the final version, "withdraw" is replaced with "cease".

34   In the final version, Dr. King replaces "the myth of time" with "the myth concerning time in relation to the struggle for freedom".

35   In the final version, the question is restated as a statement, "but it is possible that you are in too great a religious hurry."

36   In the final version, "the strangely irrational notion" becomes "the strangely rational notion".

37   In the final version, "vitriolic" is replaced by "hateful".

38   In the final version, "persistent work" is deleted.

39   In the final version, "forever realize" is replaced by "in the knowledge that".

40   In the final version, "contemporary frustration" is deleted.

41   "Incurable 'devil'" is replaced in the final version by "incorrigible 'devil'".

42   In the final version "entered" is replaced by "became an integral part of".

43   In the final version "cosmic" is replaced by "great".

44   In the final version, "sit-ins" is deleted.

45   "They will come out in ominous expressions of violence" is replaced in the final version by "they will seek expression through violence".

46   In the final version, this paragraph's final line becomes the first line of the next paragraph. It is slightly changed to "But though I was initially disappointed at being categorized as an extremist, as I continued to think about the matter…"

47   In the final version, "and persecute you" is added.

48   In the final version "gospel of Jesus Christ" is replaced by "Christian gospel."

49   In the final version the word "extremist" is not repeated with reference to Bunyan, Lincoln, Jefferson.

50   Final version adds "need".

51   "Or appreciate" is deleted in the final version.

52   In the final version, Dr. King adds the names of Ann Braden and Sarah Patton Boyle. See notes 99 and 100 respectively.

53   "And understanding" is deleted in the final version.

54   "Angry" is deleted in the final version.

55   "Let me rush on to mention" is replaced by "Let me take note of" in the final version.

56   In the final version Dr. King adds the adjective "major".

57   Dr. King deleted "I had the strange feeling" in the final version. He writes instead, "When I was suddenly catapulted into the leadership of the bus protest in Montgomery, Alabama, a few years ago, I felt we would be supported by the white church…."

58   In the final version, "Alabama" is added.

59   "Of the past" is deleted in the final version.

60   In the final version "churches" is replaced with "churchmen".

61   In the final version, "made" is put in the present tense, "makes".

62   In the final version, Dr. King adds here the adjective, "unbiblical".

63   In the final version, Dr. King deletes this paragraph.

64   In the final version, the adjective "lofty" is added here.

65   In the final version, "outlay" is replaced by "outline".

66   In the final version "Who worships here?" is replaced by "What kind of people worship here?"

67   In the final version "tired" is deleted.

68   In the final version, "I love her sacred walls" is deleted.

69   In the final version "nonconformist" is put in the plural, "nonconformists".

70   In the final version "they" is replaced with "Christians".

71   The final version reads, "By their effort and example they brought an end…."

72   The final puts "contest" in the plural, "contests".

73   The final version changes "arch-supporter" to "archdefender".

74   The final version adds the word "even" here.

75   In the final version "authentic ring" is replaced by "authenticity".

76   This sentence is deleted in the final version.

77   This sentence is deleted in the final version.

78   In the final version, "kicked out of" is replaced by "dismissed from".

79   This sentence is deleted in the final version.

80   In the final version, "foreparents" is replaced by "forebears".

81   In the final version "in the midst of brutal injustice" is replaced by "while suffering gross injustice".

82   This sentence is deleted in the final version.

83   The specifics of the confrontation with the Birmingham police are made less specific in the final version. Thus "…if you had seen its angry violent dogs literally biting six unarmed, nonviolent

Negroes" is replaced with "…if you had seen its dogs sinking their teeth into unarmed, nonviolent Negroes."

84   In the final version, "Negro" is deleted.

85   In the final version, "I'm sorry that" is deleted.

86   In the final version "flagrant" is replaced with "racial".

87   In the final version, Dr. King gives the precise quote, "As T. S. Eliot has said: 'The last temptation is the greatest treason: To do the right deed for the wrong reason.'"

88   In the final version "the most inhuman provocation" is replaced by "in the midst of great provocation".

89   In the final version "courageously and with a majestic sense of purpose" is replaced by "with the noble sense of purpose".

90   In the final version "thus carrying our whole nation" is replaced by "thereby bringing our nation".

91   In the final version this parenthetical statement is deleted.

92   In the final version "alone for days in the dull monotony of a narrow jail cell" is replaced by "alone in a narrow jail cell".

93   In the final version "strange" is replaced by "long".

94   In the final version "having a patience that makes me patient with anything less than brotherhood" is replaced by "having a patience that allows me to settle for anything less than brotherhood".

95   In the final version "tomorrow" is replaced by "future".

OTHER LITERATURE BY PETER A. LILLBACK

available at www.ProvidenceForum.org

Philadelphia Faith and Freedom Curriculum
(Includes Philadelphia Guide Book and the Guided Tour on DVD)
Almost everyone knows that Philadelphia is a city rich in history. But far too few know how much Philadelphia's history is interconnected with the Bible. This curriculum, suitable for lower and upper grades, accompanies the Philadelphia Faith and Freedom Tour Guide, the Providence Forum's exciting tour of America's Founding City where faith and freedom work together to forge American liberty. The curriculum, which is aligned with the Common Core Standards, groups all 52 sites from the Philadelphia Faith & Freedom Tour in chronological order and presents it in 23 lessons. The Curriculum is supported by a walking tour DVD of Dr. Lillback visiting 20 of the sites. Currently (2012) being taught in several elementary and secondary schools, it is available and suitable for homeschool and conventional classrooms. Order today to discover that the Bible and its Judeo-Christian message are still important today even as they were for the beginning of our country.

George Washington & Israel
Dr. Lillback's insightful work researches the question, "Is it inherently American to be pro-Israel?" While it is true Israel did not exist in Washington's day, in fact, the British Balfour Declaration of 1917 began the process of establishing Israel 130 years after the US Constitution was written. Yet, could the evidence from Washington's life and writings show that he knew far more about Israel than most thought possible? Within its pages, Dr. Lillback answers that question and reveals what other American presidents have to say on this very timely topic.

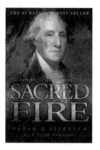

George Washington's Sacred Fire

What sets the national bestseller *George Washington's Sacred Fire* apart from all previous works on this man for the ages, is the exhaustive fifteen years of Dr. Lillback's research, revealing a unique icon driven by the highest of ideals. Only do George Washington's own writings, journals, letters, manuscripts, and those of his closest family and confidants reveal the truth of this awe-inspiring role model for all generations.

Dr. Lillback paints a picture of a man, who, faced with unprecedented challenges and circumstances, ultimately drew upon his persistent qualities of character – honesty, justice, equity, perseverance, piety, forgiveness, humility, and servant leadership, to become one of the most revered figures in world history.

George Washington set the cornerstone for what would become one of the most prosperous, free nations in the history of civilization. Through this book, Dr. Lillback, assisted by Jerry Newcombe, reveals to the reader a newly inspirational image of General and President George Washington.

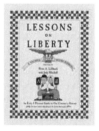

Lessons on Liberty: A Primer for Young Patriots

Designed for all ages and packed with colorful illustrations, this entertaining and educational hardcover book uses a simple alphabet poem to guide the reader through the fundamental principles of American liberty. Co-authored by Judy Mitchell, the book incorporates early nineteenth century dictionary definitions and enhanced graphics, Bible quotations and *Poor Richard's Almanack*, this engaging book adds powerful historic quotes, surprising facts, and truths about our nation's founding to excite young and old about our country—this beacon of liberty for the world. Included also are activity pages to further teach young scholars with a hands-on approach—perforated for easy tear-out, these pages may be reproduced on a copier for group use. James Madison once declared, *"The diffusion of knowledge is the only guardian of true liberty."* Whether in your family, or in a public, Christian or home school setting, please join us in striving to preserve our unparalleled heritage of freedom for future generations by introducing them to these timeless truths.

Freedom's Holy Light...
With A Firm Reliance On Divine Providence

The flagship publication of The Providence Forum, this easy to read, thirty-five-page booklet recaps America's Judeo-Christian heritage in the foundations and ongoing development of our nation. It presents the stories of the very first covenants of the colonies, leading to and including the Declaration of Independence, The Constitution, The Great Seal of the United States, our flag, the Pledge of Allegiance, our national motto and more. *Freedom's Holy Light* has been distributed coast to coast by individuals, at political and community leadership conferences, religious and homeschool networks, radio stations, Christian schools, and bookstores. *Freedom's Holy Light* is endorsed by, among others, Dr. John DiIulio, former Director of the White House Office of Faith-based and Community Initiatives, US Congressman Joe Pitts, Anthony Cardinal Bevilacqua, and Rabbi Daniel Lapin. This book is as entertaining as it is educational, illuminating the intersection of our Judeo-Christian faith, national history and government. The success of America is still dependent upon what our founders described as a "firm reliance on Divine Providence."

A Tour of the Dollar Bill

One of the most profound tools of influence in our society, indeed in the world, is the almighty American dollar. Remarkably, the one-dollar bill has a story to tell about the history and founding principles of our nation, the men that have steered her course since, and our historic symbols and institutions. It reveals the distinctive principles of America, as determined by our founders. The dollar bill explains the founding faith and values of our nation in various ways, including outlining seven essential moral virtues and recognizing the role of Providence in the formation of our nation. Based on Dr. Lillback's renowned presentation seen around the world, Providence Forum Press designed a careful, but non-exact, replica of the one dollar bill with a written "tour" of America's history as told by Dr. Lillback and the dollar itself. Sadly, people are largely ignorant of the history they handle on a daily basis. This entertaining and educational tool fits in any wallet, just as the authentic dollar does, and can be used in many ways to spread the much forgotten history of America's providential founding.

The Folding Flag

This unique educational tool teaches you how to fold the American flag, and the meaning of each fold as described by the Air Force Academy. Learn the history and significance of each of the 12 folds as this paper flag is transformed into George Washington's hat.

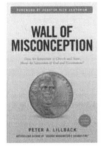

Wall of Misconception

The "wall of separation between church and state" is a phrase not found anywhere in the Constitution, but activist judges have recklessly used that phrase to stamp out public religious expression. We are restricted from praying in public schools, the Ten Commandments and other religious symbols have been stripped from public buildings, and the term "under God" in the Pledge of Allegiance has been called "unconstitutional". Dr. Peter Lillback exposes the church/state separation myth that has led to such actions in his groundbreaking book entitled *Wall of Misconception*. Within its pages, Lillback counters the claims that Christianity must only reside in the walls of the church by pointing to America's Founding Fathers and historical documents that prove Christianity's incontrovertible influence on our nation at large.